Brewer at Bay

Brewer at Bay

by

SIR PAUL NICHOLSON

Paul Nicholson

The Memoir Club

First published in 2003 by
The Memoir Club
Whitworth Hall
Spennymoor
County Durham

British Library Cataloguing in
Publication Data.
A catalogue record for this book
is available from the
British Library.

ISBN: 1 84104 069 X

Typeset by George Wishart & Associates, Whitley Bay.
Printed by Bookcraft (Bath) Ltd.

Dedication

To my wife Sarah, who has been so wonderful in the good times and such a tower of strength when they are tough, and to our daughter, Lucy.

Acknowledgements

The Rt Reverend Michael Turnbull – former Bishop of Durham – for permission to publish his sermon of 21 June 1999.

Denise Robertson and John Lowe for their help and advice.

The Journal, *The Northern Echo* and *The Sunderland Echo* for their photographs.

Contents

Illustrations

Foreword

I CAN'T REMEMBER when I first became aware of Vaux. Like family, it was always there. As a child I believed that Vaux owned every pub in the country and brewed for the nation, just as I believed Sunderland built every ship that sailed the seas. Impossible then to imagine that one day the signs would be torn down, the workforce cast adrift and a gaping hole left in the centre of Sunderland.

As I grew older I realized the significance of such a large company to a region in which employers were too often branches of larger firms with headquarters elsewhere. Vaux was a pillar of the north-east economy, its signs were everywhere and, if you had been away, when you re-entered 'Vaux territory' you knew that you were home. It was a company which operated decently, valued its workers and was keen to participate in anything that benefited the community.

Later on, when I got to know Paul Nicholson, I realized that, although he was a shrewd businessman, he cared deeply for his heritage and its role in furthering the region's interests. In 1999 I sympathized with his struggle to fend off those who wanted to destroy what he and his forbears had built. When he lost I watched in amazement as the company was torn down . . . literally torn down for, as I write, gaunt shards of steel and masonry are all that remain of the building that was once its hub.

The people of the North East are used to closure and subsequent unemployment because of prevailing economic conditions. The burning question, in the case of Vaux, is whether the decision to sell out was based on economic necessity or corporate greed. As the story unfolded in the press it was difficult not to feel that an element of spite had entered in . . . and yet it seemed impossible that any reputable business man or woman could behave in such a fashion.

Sir Paul has written an honest, and often scathing, account of the death of Vaux but he gives us much more than that. This is the story of an idyllic childhood, a privileged youth and a successful business career which culminated in a bitter boardroom battle. There are fascinating glimpses behind the scenes at the Coronation, tales of travel and sport and details of his extensive public service but it is in his recounting of the battle for Vaux that his passion shines through. I'm proud to write the foreword to a book which not only entertains but answers questions people in the North East and the business world beyond have pondered for too long.

Denise Robertson

Preface

WHEN I WAS approached by the Memoir Club some two years ago with the suggestion I should consider writing my own memoirs, I was, to begin with, sceptical about such an undertaking. I have been lucky to enjoy a more varied life of work and play than most, but I thought it rather conceited to believe others would be particularly interested. However, there is one story which I very much wanted to tell. It is a story which impacted adversely on the lives of hundreds of people in the North East and Sheffield and it is a story of something which should not have happened. Chapter 10 tells this story under the heading 'Death of Vaux'.

The publisher suggested that the best way to put this story into context would be by writing about my whole life. I was encouraged by the comments of those who read earlier drafts, to go ahead and publish.

My whole adult career after finishing education and training was with Vaux Group based in Sunderland. Vaux Group was one of the few substantial independent companies in the North East. I have some pride in my record during the 27 years I was Chief Executive, combining this role with that of Chairman for 22 of those years. For my final six months I was Non Executive Chairman. During my time in charge, the Group each year paid a higher dividend on its shares than the year before and apart from the years 1991-1994 during a hotel recession, always made record profits.

The heart of Vaux which was founded by my Grandmother's Grandfather, Cuthbert Vaux, in 1837 was in brewing, but it had also successfully developed the Swallow Hotel chain.

Throughout my career, I believed that the long term interests of the shareholders were best served by keeping the company independent. I devoted a great deal of time and effort to trying to keep potential predators away. The title of my book comes from the headline of an article in the *Guardian* newspaper in the eighties, 'Brewer at Bay'. While my personal shareholding was less than one half of one percent of the total, my holding did represent the major portion of my own net worth.

As Chief Executive of a significant North East company which depended for so much of its profits on its North East customers, I found myself involved in many of the initiatives to improve the region's economy over the last three decades of the twentieth century. To date there is no other person who has served both as Chairman of the CBI Northern Region and President of the North East Chamber of Commerce. I hope that an insider view of some of these initiatives will be of historical interest to some, particularly in regard to the Tyne and Wear Development Corporation and the Northern Development Company.

I resigned from the Vaux Group (by then renamed Swallow Group) on 26th March 1999, a week after the board had accepted advice from a London Corporate Financier to reject a management offer to buy Vaux Breweries, leading inevitably to their closure and the loss of many hundreds of jobs in Sunderland and Sheffield. I had repeatedly warned my then colleagues in the weeks leading up to my resignation that this advice was grossly flawed, as it can now be shown to have been.

There was a lot of pontificating by the directors and others at the time about 'Corporate Governance' at Vaux. The first requirement of good corporate governance should be competence. In this respect what was done to Vaux Breweries was a gross miscarriage of corporate governance amounting in effect to 'Corporate Vandalism'.

Chapter 1

The Early Years

I HAD A PRIVILEGED start in life without being too privileged. My roots are firmly in the North of England, where there have been Nicholsons in County Durham for a number of centuries. A genealogical book on the family trees of Nicholsons, traces my branch back eight generations to George Nicholson, who must have been born in the 17th century, as there is a record of his son Richard's marriage at St Mary-le-Bow Durham in 1731. Richard's second son, also George, was Architect to the Dean and Chapter, Durham Cathedral and built Prebends Bridge in Durham. However my ancestor was Richard's third son Joseph, a mason, whose own son Thomas followed his uncle George as Architect to the Dean and Chapter of Durham Cathedral. My grandfather's grandfather evidently moved to Sunderland and started a shipping business, which was run subsequently by my great grandfather Henry. This business apparently folded around 1910 so that he ended up as a pensioner of his own son and my grandfather, Frank, born in 1875.

As a family we have speculated whether the earliest traced of our branch – George – was any relation of James Nicholson, who lived at West Rainton some 5 miles east of Durham around the same time. George's son had married in 1731. Some 5 years later James's daughter and heiress Jean married Thomas Lyon, 8th Earl of Strathmore. It was their son John who married Mary Bowes, daughter and heiress of George Bowes – hence the Bowes Lyons. It is not generally known that the Earls of Strathmore are descended on the distaff side from not one but two Durham heiresses.

My grandfather, who became Sir Frank Nicholson in 1943, was an outstanding businessman. He left Sunderland High School at the age of 16, and then trained as a Chartered Accountant, passing his exams in the top two of his year. He married in 1899 Miss Amy Vaux, and my father, Douglas, was born in 1905. Amy's two brothers were the owners of the Sunderland brewers C. Vaux & Sons, which had been founded by their grandfather Cuthbert in 1837. They recruited my grandfather, who from then on took a major part in the running of the company and its development, although he was never allowed by his brothers-in-law to own any shares in the company until it was merged in 1927 with the considerably larger North Eastern Breweries, and became public. Originally the merged company was to have the inspiring name of 'The Associated Breweries', however for marketing reasons, Grandfather persuaded his colleagues to add the name Vaux and the company was known as Vaux and Associated Breweries until the 1970s. While Vaux was managed by three generations of Nicholsons for over 100 years, we never had a significant holding in the company. The Vaux family still had a shareholding, when I joined, of around 10%, but this was little protection from takeover unless we could keep performance up.

On my mother's side the Tancreds had lived in the same area of Yorkshire since the 12th century. They had become Baronets in 1662. However in the 19th century they fell on hard times and emigrated to New Zealand, where my great grandfather was born. He subsequently was a distinguished engineer at the end of that century responsible for, among other projects, the Forth Rail Bridge and the Yukon Railway. His son was known as 'Tiger Tom' because of his appetite for shooting tigers while in the Indian Army. He was in the churchyard of the village of Aldborough by Boroughbridge looking for graves of his ancestors when he met a Yorkshire heiress 20 years his junior. They were married and in the fashion of the time, her name, Lawson, was hyphenated with his. He thus returned to his roots. My mother, Pauline, their third child, was born in 1916.

In 1937 Douglas Nicholson married Pauline Lawson-Tancred and I was born a year later, just as the storm clouds preceding the war were gathering. I was lucky to survive a major operation for a

1939 (Dec), in front of Quarry Hill with the dogs.

kidney stone the next year, but have no recollection of this other than a large scar. Very earliest memories for me are of living for a time in Prestwich and then Tickhill, South Yorkshire, where my mother had taken accommodation to be near my father, who at the outbreak of war had been mobilized with his regiment – the Scottish Horse. My brother Nigel was born in June 1940 but I do not have clear recollections of the time before my father went abroad in 1942. He was to be away nearly three years. Thus my mother, still under 26, was left bringing up two small boys. She was far from alone in this situation and like thousands of others she just had to cope. We continued to live at Quarry Hill which my parents had rented from the Brancepeth Estate and where I had been born. Quarry Hill dates from Elizabethan times and was originally the dower house of the estate, which in 1940 still ran to some twelve thousand acres and belonged to Lord Boyne head of the Hamilton Russell family who had a seat at Brancepeth Castle. During the war the castle became the headquarters of the Durham Light Infantry training depot.

Attached to Quarry Hill was a small farm of forty acres where we had chickens and two milk cows, so we always had fresh eggs and butter made at home by hand churn. Such luxuries were precious in days of food rationing. We certainly did not suffer hunger although I am told that I was once found eating our Welsh Corgi Taffy's dog biscuits. Mother for a time worked as a landgirl, and my brother and I enjoyed rides on the tractor with her. This of course was some 40 years before the Health and Safety Executive.

Petrol was short but my mother's soft-top Austin 7 seemed to be there when needed. There was also the pony, Polly, and trap to take us to the village, while the railway station was only some 400 yards away with frequent little steam trains into Durham Station, where one could change onto a Chester-le-Street train which stopped at the end of Grandfather's back drive. Sunday lunch, with 'Grandpa and Gran' was a special treat. 'Sir Frank' had bought the Southill Estate near Chester-le-Street in 1926, and lived in the Hall. The house had originally been designed by the famous local architect John Dobson, but had been considerably enlarged subsequently. Grandmother had had a bad fall in the early 1940s and was an invalid living with a nurse, with her bedroom on the ground floor. I can remember being taken to nearby Lumley Castle where Sir Roger Lumley, who had been Governor of an Indian state, lived. Sir Roger – who subsequently inherited the Earldom of Scarbrough – was held in some awe by my grand-parents, as were the newly married Lord and Lady Lambton, heir to the Earldom of Durham, whom I remember coming to lunch.

In 1944 I started school at an old fashioned dame's school in Durham, 'Miss Derry's'. Miss Derry was a spinster lady of a certain age. There were not many pupils and most lived within walking distance so could go home for lunch. In my case she would take me to the 'British Restaurant' for a plain but filling lunch. I didn't learn much. I couldn't master reading taught by the word recognition method, although I showed an aptitude for sums. We used only pencils for writing.

At Quarry Hill, we were in sight of some half dozen pit heaps. A source of endless fascination was the overhead bucket line crossing our back lane transporting coal from New Brancepeth some three miles to the coking mills at Willington. There was far more pollution then. Quarry Hill windows were frequently covered with a pall of coal dust, while coal fires burning in every cottage or terrace house created a cloud, which even in the north sometimes became a smog, although the pea soupers endured further south were rare. I can't say I suffered wartime privation. What one had not experienced, one didn't miss. The war itself hardly impinged, despite my father's absence, although I was aware of the death of two uncles, one a soldier married to my father's sister, the other a bomber pilot and my mother's eldest brother. I can remember while staying with my mother's family hearing a roar and a crash outside, as a flak damaged bomber, limping back to base, hit a tree opposite the house, but it didn't actually crash until it had gone some hundreds of yards further. I remember the next day that my brother and I picked up various bits of debris from the plane. The towns of the North East, particularly near the coast, suffered their share of bombing, but we were well inland.

I knew my father when he came home in January 1945 mainly from his photograph. He had managed to return early because Vaux needed him, as my grandfather, by now aged 70, was finding it hard to cope.

When my grandfather joined the company nearly 50 years earlier, he made Vaux famous for its Stout, which was sold all over Britain. In the years before the First World War the company had depots in Glasgow, Leeds and Burton-on-Trent. However during that war delivery restrictions were introduced which meant that English Breweries had major problems delivering outside the region where they were located. Guinness being an Irish Brewery was not subject to the same restrictions and used the opportunity of the war years to establish a near total dominance of the national Stout market. Under the first Lord Iveagh they were far ahead of their time in understanding the importance of marketing and advertising, particularly with the slogan 'Guinness is good for you'.

The First World War coincided with the height of the temperance movement. The 'demon drink' was held responsible for productivity problems in the armament factories, so much so that to control the problem the Government nationalized the pub and beer trade around Carlisle and Invergordon in Scotland. They then attempted to persuade the whole industry to agree to being nationalized. Family legend has it that this was only prevented by my grandfather leading an effective revolt against such a move within the ranks of the brewers, after the industry leadership had virtually capitulated.

In 1919, because of the demand in the North East for Scottish Beer, Grandfather had tried to persuade his brothers in law to buy a Scottish Brewery and when they declined, bought to his own account Lorimer and Clark's Caledonian Brewery in Edinburgh. The Lorimer brand of 'Scotch' was for many years famous throughout the region. Southerners entering a Vaux pub and asking for a 'Scotch' would be surprised to be served a glass of beer rather than the hard stuff.

My Father had joined the company aged 22, straight from University, in 1927. He had not intended this but my grandfather required him in the company to balance the interests of C. Vaux and Sons alongside the somewhat larger Sunderland Brewery they were merging with, which belonged to the Murray family and was known as 'North Eastern Breweries'. Father then cut his teeth in the company during the depression. Sunderland is only a few miles from Jarrow, from where the famous march started, and was to know periods of great hardship until the economy picked up in the late thirties as a result of rearmament and an expanding demand for shipping.

In some ways it was ironic that another major North East recession coincided with my early days in the company, although the welfare state mitigated to some degree the worst affects. Sunderland alongside other parts of the North East was to be hit by a series of economic blows during my time, particularly with the collapse of shipbuilding and coal mining. I, along with many other businessmen operating in such a climate could not help being moved by a desire to do what they could for the region. In my case it was not altruistic, as what was good for the region was good for Vaux which had its heart in the North East, although over time it developed national interests, particularly through Swallow Hotels.

When Father returned from the War, he was to face considerable problems getting the company moving forward again. One of these problems which must have been highly fraught for both him and his father, followed the appointment by my grandfather of a Labour Peer to the Board. This may have been because at the time (1945) it looked as if Labour would be there for a long time or it may have been an early attempt at good 'Corporate Governance', although such a phrase was unknown until many years later. Anyhow this new director then tried to organize a coup to oust my Father and Grandfather, alleging that they had acted improperly because Grandfather had in 1946 sold Lorimers Brewery which he had bought in the early twenties to the company. Grandfather, who was the most upright of men, would never have dreamt of doing anything improper but the directors decided on an investigation by a leading QC into the allegations. The QC found the allegations of impropriety totally without foundation. My grandfather and father were completely exonerated. The peer departed from the board. None of this ever became public. It was long before the days of aggressive financial journalism and excessive 'Corporate Governance'.

However there is some irony in that over fifty years later, the downfall of the company resulted in part from a similar attempt at political correctness in board appointments.

Father was a formidable man. One of the most brilliant horsemen of his generation, he was passionate about riding. He also was a substantial businessman in his own right and expected high standards from his family. He was appalled at my lack of reading skills and personally took the matter in hand, teaching me to read phonetically, so that I soon caught up to where I should be. He stood as Conservative Candidate for Spennymoor constituency in the 1945 election in which along with most other Tories he was soundly defeated. That was the end of any political aspirations he had, and the rest of his career was spent running Vaux, until as a

1945, Nigel, Father and myself behind.

result of a near fatal head injury from a fall from a horse in the nineteen-thirties, he suffered Alzheimer's disease some forty years later.

It is hard for the present generation to imagine the world of 1945. The country was on its knees economically. It was the era of steam trains which took over five hours for the journey from Durham to London, although after the Hatfield rail accident some of us were reminded of what this was like! The A1 road from the North to London wound through Darlington, Leeming, and Boroughbridge with a real bottleneck at Doncaster and then through a number of other towns and villages. It was a 7-hour drive if there was petrol. On the other hand, the doctor came to visit as a matter of course those who were sick. There were still, in most well-to-do homes, maids and in some cases butlers. This was in spite of taxation of income at 19/6d in the £ and death duties of 80%. Many small luxuries had disappeared during the war years. I can recall for instance the excitement in 1945 of being given a banana for the first time.

After Father returned life looked up. He was determined that my brother and I should learn to ride horses well. He still had two of his prewar hunters, while we rode 'Polly', the highland pony who had pulled our wartime trap, and 'Glen', her son. These two ponies were brilliant children's rides.

In 1946 my parents took me on a trip to Ireland as a pre prep school treat. There we stayed with the legendary horseman, Joe Dudgeon. He had commanded my father's regiment, the Scottish Horse. We motored some thousand miles round Ireland, and I remember being firmly told not to talk about this. They didn't want questions on how enough petrol was found in such a fuel-starved era!

Possibly the greatest shock to the system was in September 1946. I was due to go to a local prep school Aysgarth but somewhere my father met the legendary Alan Barber, Headmaster of Ludgrove School in Berkshire and I ended up being taken there some 300 miles from home at the age of 8½. Once there, there was no question of ringing up home. Parents visited once or twice a term and small boys were left to sink or swim. Initially I sank. Ludgrove consisted at that time of some 100 boys of whom 90% were destined for Eton. I was immediately an oddball. I was destined for Harrow. Just post-war discipline was not properly enforced, although beatings by the head were frequent. Boys exhibited with pride their bruised behinds, having been exhorted by the headmaster to 'take it like a man'. Bullying was rife and I endured my share of this. The school was full of scions of the peerage from a royal duke (Kent) through marquesses, earls etc. A number of boys had lost fathers in the war and a surprising number also came from broken homes.

I was considered not tough enough and therefore was put down for boxing, which I loathed. In class, while I fared reasonably well and my first report described me as 'a boy who ought to go far', I was held back in that I had never learnt to write other than with a pencil and was hopelessly untidy with ink. There was one saving grace – the greatest teacher I was ever to experience, K.B. Morrison, (K.B.M.) was a bachelor Old

Harrovian, who took under his wing boys who were going to that establishment. My reports speak of friction with my contemporaries because I was inclined to speak my mind and not go along with the crowd. Gradually for me things improved and at the end I passed common entrance well into Harrow.

One has few friends from Ludgrove days, among my direct contemporaries were Charlie Douglas Home, who sadly died very early when he was editor of *The Times*, David Bathurst who also died early, and Paul Foot. Paul was a real maverick. He arrived at the age of 10, when the rest had arrived at 8 and – shock horror! – claimed to be a Liberal, when no other boy would admit to being other than a Conservative and most were probably well to the right of Genghis Khan. I am afraid his Ludgrove experiences shifted him even further off to the left, and almost at times off the political spectrum. I have not seen him from the day I left in 1951, but I have followed his career with interest.

It is surprising how few of those I knew at Ludgrove I have subsequently come across. Looking down the list for July 1947, there are fewer than ten. Alick Rankin, who was to become Chairman of Scottish and Newcastle before sadly dying far too young, is the only old Ludgrovian who was a close friend in later life. There were one or two others who are good acquaintances, but many Ludgrovians were of a rather different social stratum from myself and regarded themselves as very superior! One exception was Alastair Stewart, who became in fairly short order Viscount Castlereagh, then the Marquis of Londonderry. He had a family home, Wynyard, in Durham where as a small boy I stayed several times. He had two rather older, but to a small boy, very beautiful sisters Jane (Rayne) one of the Queen's Maids of Honour at the Coronation and Annabel (Birley then Goldsmith) after whom the Berkeley Square nightclub is named. Alastair's father was particularly memorable, as he would always give me a £1 note when he saw me (a 1950 £1 note is the equivalent of £20 today!) I haven't seen Alastair since he left Durham after selling Wynyard to the property developer Sir John Hall some 15 years ago, but we keep in touch at Christmas.

1950, Ludgrove 1st eleven football team, PDN right front, brother Nigel second from right rear.

Ludgrove was very much a sporting school and team games were never my strong point. I had an accident, cutting tendons in both my wrists, when my brother slammed a glass panel door and I put my hands up. After that I was never happy with bat or racquet, although I made captain of Ludgrove 2nd XI cricket and was also in the first XI football. I won a number of prizes at Ludgrove mainly for the piano, which I am afraid I gave up at Harrow as it was so boringly taught. Today I couldn't play a note. My strong points educationally were at the time maths, but under the teaching of K.B.M., I came to appreciate the classics and the English language. In the common entrance exam for Harrow I was marked 100% for divinity – they may have thought there was a potential priest coming, if so they were soon disappointed!

The years 8 to 13 are probably very important to one's long term character development. In my case some of the influences of Ludgrove were positive but some negative. The shock of finding out that not everyone in the world was nice, and some were definitely nasty, developed a certain aggressiveness as a form of defence and this is coupled with shyness. I am not a particularly good mixer with people nor wildly sociable and, while I have a small select number of close friends, I am not inclined to trust easily. Ludgrove was also very elitist. It took a long time to realize that people less fortunate than myself were not necessarily inferior!

I went on to Harrow in 1951, the year their greatest old boy, Winston Churchill, returned as Prime Minister. In Harrow's case he literally returned almost every year from 1940 until his death in 1965. He came for a concert of the Harrow songs which had been written largely around the time he had been there and were very much a feature of Harrow tradition. Such titles as 'Forty Years On', 'Ducker', 'Stet Fortuna Domus' and some 20 others – with words and music by Harrow masters of long ago, still are very emotional to almost all Old Harrovians and were particularly so to Churchill.

In 1951 some of the spartan days of public schools were still very much alive. While morning cold baths were no longer obligatory, it was the privilege of a boy who had been there two years to be allowed the privacy of closing the door when he went to the loo. It was the privilege only of school monitors and those who had passed the Dolphin test, (swimming a mile in a set time), to be allowed to wear bathing costumes in the magnificent 170 yard long open air pool called 'Ducker', where many happy hot summer afternoons could be spent. This went on for years, until the school became aware that paedophile voyeurs could witness this scene from the top deck of passing buses. The head of each of the 11 houses could beat junior boys with the housemaster's permission for a range of minor offences. This privilege was exercised with some gusto by the more sadistic of heads, although I don't think homosexuality was a serious issue. A certain amount of clandestine mutual masturbation went on, but not a great deal else. It was not a subject that was thought about in the fifties. Most boys were far more interested in sport, work or their hobbies. Some did develop an interest in the opposite sex, and one head of house was forced to leave after being caught 'in flagrante' with a maid.

New boys for their first few terms were 'fags'. Any sixth former (House monitor) wanting an errand doing, stood in the hall and yelled 'Boy, Boy, Boy' at which all fags had to run to the call, the last one getting the job. In addition each sixth former had his own personal fag who cleaned his shoes, made his bed and laid his fire. It was a fairly tough life, but in contrast to Ludgrove there was little bullying.

Harrow was split into Houses each with their own Housemaster, but unlike at Eton, the House was known by its location and not by its Housemaster. While my father had been in the 'Headmaster's', he sent all his five sons to 'Elmfield'. This House, under its previous Housemaster Cyril Browne, had dominated competitive sport in cricket (summer term), in rugby (winter term), and Harrow football (Easter term). Cyril Browne had died some 3 years before I went and had been replaced by Ronald Watkins, a classical scholar and a great Shakespearian expert, who did not have the same attitude to sport.

While I was there we had two Middle East Kings – Faisal of Iraq, sadly assassinated shortly after leaving, and Hussein of Jordan who was in my form. He arrived shortly after his grandfather had been assassinated, with Hussein beside him taking a bullet on the medal he was wearing on his chest. Hussein was not there more than a few terms, but developed a great love of the school in latter years and was a generous benefactor.

Filling the gossip columns of the time were mothers of two contemporaries. Lady Docker whose husband, Sir Bernard, was Chairman of Daimler, had a special Daimler covered in gold leaf. There was also Barbara Cartland. She was less ostentatious but more formidable. Her son Ian was an exact contemporary and has remained a good friend. Both these ladies made frequent visits bringing their complacent husbands with them. Almost every week Barbara would be in the House leaving husband Hugh McCorquodale sitting outside in the chauffeur's seat.

Having passed into 'Remove', which apart from scholarships boys was the top stream, my progress up the school was pedestrian rather than distinguished. Reports tell of my untidiness and lack of sociability, but also praise my diligence and general ability. In sport, unlike my brother Nigel who joined me there two years later, I was never a star. I was a run of the mill rugby and Harrow football player and, until I gave it up in favour of rifle shooting, an undistinguished cricketer. I did continue for a time taking piano lessons, but gave these up, to the fury of my father with whom I had one of the few serious rows of my life, when he accused me of lacking will and perseverance.

I avoided the cane myself. Not many did in my first year, where Robert Dickinson who came from the North and is now a friend, was a particularly fierce disciplinarian as Head of House. In my third year Roddy Bloomfield one of the more enlightened Heads of House abolished the two-year rule in the loo.

I had one unique and unforgettable experience at the time. My father in 1939, just before the war, had been given the 'Venture' stage coach and four grey horses by Louis Priestman, a famous 'Whip', as amateur drivers of coaches are known, and a major coal owner. He had for years driven this coach between Shotley Bridge and Newcastle mainly for his pleasure. When war broke out, these horses were in the brewery and used alongside the heavy horses for local beer delivery. After the war, my father bought several more grey hunters and continued, albeit intermittently, driving. In February 1952 the King had died. My grandfather also died that year in December. When plans for the coronation came to be made, it was realized there was a serious shortage of horses to pull the Empire (yes there still was one!) and Commonwealth dignitaries due to take part in the processions. The Coaching Club which had been founded in 1871 and consisted of members driving teams of horses to private coaches known as 'Park Drags', was approached. Post war the club was far from active but had just survived, and having been resuscitated in 1950, was tasked with finding horses for the ten carriage procession of Commonwealth Prime Ministers. There was an added incentive that the owners of coaches, if they were also 'Whips', could drive. Father agreed to lend five horses and asked if I could be his footman. After some quibbling at the idea of a 15 year old, this was agreed. I had to be fitted out with royal livery of scarlet and gold and with a gold bordered top hat, but most of this was available from previous coronations. As I was reasonably tall for my age, there was little problem fitting both of us out. The Coronation was set for June 2nd, but the horses were required for training and rehearsal from April. They were stabled at the Royal Mews, the name of the stables for Buckingham Palace. The initial training was a disaster. We were taken to Woolwich and required to try and drive through narrow lanes of soldiers banging dustbin lids. This terrified the horses so much, that most of them were too unsettled for any more training, and could take no part in the Coronation. We were reduced to bringing down two of the original pre-war horses, by now aged 26 each, as replacements.

We had two actual rehearsals of the procession in May, held soon after 4 a.m. for which I had special leave from school. Then the great day dawned, we were to be number six in the procession driving Dr Malan of South Africa. Winston Churchill was in the

1953, Coronation, Footman to Father driving Dr Malan of South Africa.

front carriage, followed by Canada, Australia, India and New Zealand. The crowds had been lining all parts of the route for days. The previous evening we had had supper in Piccadilly with people already lined up thick. At around 8 a.m. on the day, we drove from the Mews to the Palace and collected our passengers, before setting off down the Mall past Horse Guards to the Abbey. Our carriage was greeted with few cheers and a lot of boos. South Africa was already something of a pariah state. Each time Dr Malan heard boos he slammed up the window of the carriage and was in a foul temper when he arrived, not even acknowledging me as I opened his door for him.

After dropping our passengers, Father had arranged hospitality for the 'whips' and their footmen in offices in Deans Yard. These were owned by the Brewers Society as headquarters for their parliamentary lobbying operation. We based ourselves there, and were then able to find our way back, close to the Abbey entrance to watch the other processions arriving, including finally the Queen in her state coach. It was a glittering sight, although the weather was turning increasingly wet. After she arrived, we returned to Deans Yard for refreshments, then Father found an Abbey entrance with an obliging official, who on being asked was there any place from where we could see what was going on, took us into a top gallery from where we could look down on the whole proceedings. We possibly had the best view in the Abbey of the Queen being crowned and of mitres and magnificent military uniforms, including Churchill wearing the uniform of Lord Warden of the Cinq Ports. After spending an hour or so up there, we went back to prepare for the return procession by which time it was raining steadily. Unlike the drive to the Abbey in the morning, the return was one procession over a much longer route to give the crowds more chance to view.

We were again booed consistently and the procession got in a muddle, as the front was going too slowly and the Queen's coach could not be allowed to stop. We were therefore doubled up. This upset Churchill who pulled out, watched some go past, and then ordered his driver to take him back to Downing Street. We eventually arrived back at the Palace, dropped our passenger who was in no better mood, before returning soaked through and very cold, to the Mews. That evening we watched a firework display from a boat on the Thames but I don't recall much about this.

There can be few people alive today who had a better view of the Coronation. For my pains I received a coronation medal, and thus I was almost unique in my Harrow cadet corps and then national service days in having a ribbon on my uniform. This provoked a certain amount of jealousy, particularly when subsequently I was a guard's recruit, and few of the serving soldiers who had endured line duty on the day had been similarly rewarded.

My progression up the school was steady but far from spectacular. In those days there was a four-day exeat for 'Lords', the Eton and Harrow cricket match. Otherwise only in special circumstances were boys allowed off the Hill. Parental visits were confined to watching sport with meals either in the Kings Head, the only hotel on the Hill, or one of the tea rooms of which 'The

Hill', owned I believe by the school, was the largest. Although serving indifferent fayre, it was at least better tasting than 'house food'. I suffered badly from acne in my later teens and had to go on a rigorous and unpleasant diet, which improved matters only slightly, but which did get my weight down. This was to become useful subsequently in my competitive riding days. I did achieve the shooting eight in my final year for which I was awarded a 'Shooting Scarf', otherwise I had an undistinguished sporting record.

On the academic side, for anyone considering university it was 'Oxbridge' or nowhere. I cannot remember any contemporary going to what were patronizingly described as 'red brick universities'. My father had been at Clare College, Cambridge, whose Master Sir Henry Thirkill had been my father's tutor. He had a policy to favour the sons if he liked the father. However, I like to think that I might have passed in anyway. I was considered good enough to take the scholarship exam rather than the ordinary entrance exam. In those days if taking A levels, one only needed to do two of them, and they were not graded, other than pass and fail. Admission to 'Oxbridge' depended on interview and entrance exam. While I did not achieve a scholarship I was offered a place for 1958, but before then loomed two years of National Service.

A friend of Father's had offered to put me forward for a place in the potential officers intake (called the Brigade Squad) for the Coldstream Guards. There were however some 60 applicants for 21 places so as a reserve I was also put down for a cavalry regiment. Selection for the Brigade Squad was by the Regimental Lieutenant Colonel, Col George, later Major General Sir George, Burns DSO, MC. George Burns was a bachelor, living with his mother in Hertfordshire. I found him easy to talk to. He was particularly interested in horses and I think that was why I found myself selected to join the Brigade Squad at Caterham on September 14th 1956.

My final report from the Headmaster at Harrow contained a long apology that I had not been made a school monitor, which

1956, PDN and Paul Butler, winners of Harrow Silver Arrow Rifle shooting trophy.

had been at the time a major disappointment, particularly to my father. It may however have been a blessing in disguise, because there is no doubt that the Headmaster was sorry about this, and gave me a particularly glowing reference for the next stage of my life. The reason he gave for not making me a monitor was that in that particular year there was a surfeit of eligible candidates, and indeed there were one or two outstanding individuals. Head and shoulders above the rest was Robin (known at Harrow as Fred) Butler, a brilliant scholar, who had the unusual distinction at Oxford of getting a first class honours degree in 'Greats' and a Rugby Blue. He went on to become head of the Civil Service under Margaret Thatcher, and through the first two years of Tony Blair.

There were some outstanding masters such as Roger Ellis, subsequently Head of Marlborough and John Reay, who became Head of Westminster and much later came back into my life as Director of the Portman Group, an alcohol policy body funded by the drinks industry. The most memorable however, was Charles Lillingstone, or 'Charlie Lil'. He was a confirmed bachelor, although in his retirement he had a 'walk out' – I cannot visualize anything more – with Barbara Cartland. He taught history and was Housemaster of Druries, another of the eleven houses. He knew everybody and his speciality was placing boys at Oxbridge. His father had been a Canon at Durham Cathedral whose memorial is in the Cloisters and he always regarded Durham as his home. At his memorial service Lord Hailsham gave a moving address, describing him as the ultimate schoolmaster, a fitting tribute. No doubt in this cynical age some would question his and other bachelor masters' sexuality, but if they had any gay leanings, they were totally suppressed, and indeed many of the best schoolmasters of that era were bachelors. They did not have wives to distract them from their life vocation of teaching.

I have a few friends today whom I first came across at Harrow, particularly Robert Dickinson, a neighbour in the North East. While he was somewhat older than me, we have in recent years been associates on a number of ventures such as Tyne Tees Television and Northern Investors plc.

Of my direct contemporaries, I still see Ian MacCorquodale, Barbara Cartland's eldest son, and Tony Winlaw, who has been for many years a senior handicapper at the jockey club. Mark Dundas, as he then was, now the Marquess of Zetland, lives not far away in North Yorkshire. Mark was Head of Edenfield House when I, along with Ian MacCorquodale and Tony Winlaw, were house monitors. Mark was not a beater. There was only one occasion when he attempted to use the cane. As a fellow house monitor I was there, as we always witnessed beatings. Mark, who was a racquets player, wielded the cane with a great flourish, only to catch the overhead lampshade with a loud 'ping', at which the cane descended limply on the backside of the victim. He tried again –

same thing. He has claimed that his fellow house monitors then exhorted him to try harder, but I do not remember that!

Possibly my greatest school friend was Roger Miller, an outstanding cricketer, but in a different Harrow house called 'The Knoll'. Roger became a keen liberal and onetime Parliamentary candidate before spending many years as a prep school master at Sunningdale School. Recently we have renewed contact and he asked me to make the principal speech at a dinner in London he was hosting in the capacity of Master of the Carpenters' Company, a city livery company.

To the boarding school pupil, holidays are precious. In those days 'exeats' during term were limited. Ludgrove had none, and some terms many boys only saw their parents once. Harrow only had the annual 4-day break for the Eton and Harrow cricket match at Lords. Besides, being nearly 300 miles away, when trains were much slower and flights in their infancy, it was difficult to get home. It was quite a journey to and from school. In my case a firm called 'Universal Aunts' was deputed to conduct me across London when parents couldn't be there. Universal Aunts supplied middle-aged ladies who would meet, greet and accompany their charges between stations.

Home was always wonderful. Life consisted mostly of participating in field sports. Every summer holiday throughout my boarding school days, we spent three weeks from about the 12th August at the Lord Crewe Arms, Blanchland which Vaux leased as an early Swallow Hotel. Father rented the 'Blanchland Moor' from the Lord Crewe Trustees, a Church Charity founded by Lord Crewe an 18th century Bishop of Durham, who was also a landowner.

Unusually he shot the Moor almost exclusively over pointer dogs. The dogs roam in front of the two guns and when they scent grouse they freeze while the guns come up and flush the birds. He much preferred this method of shooting where on a good day, two or three guns might shoot 30-40 birds between them and take a lot of exercise in the process, to the more usual method of shooting grouse by 'driving'. Here beaters drive a large area towards a line of 6-9 guns hidden in 'Butts'. Nowadays, in the age of the four wheel drive vehicle, although less so in the fifties and sixties, the guns are motored from drive to drive and take very little exercise. They can kill many more grouse in the process, but often actually shoot fewer per gun and can endure a long boring wait. Father always maintained that it was not worth driving grouse unless the total bag would be at least one hundred brace (two hundred birds).

In September we shot partridges, all walked up, of which there was a profusion, both around Brancepeth where he took the shooting, and at Southill the family estate. In a good year three or four guns could expect to shoot over forty brace (eighty birds) in a day.

At the age of 15 my mother took me deer stalking for the first time. We went to Braemar near Ullapool. This belonged to John Calder who had been Chairman of Ind Coope pre-war. Calder lived to over 90, putting down his longevity to the fact that his father had believed small boys should not work too hard, so they were sent every summer for three months or more to the Highlands for fishing, shooting and related activities. He and his brother, Sir James, each had very distinguished careers. I duly shot my first stag, introducing me to what I still regard among the finest of country sports.

Pheasant shooting didn't feature strongly because it was in the middle of the fox hunting season, and that had total priority in the Christmas holidays. There is a picture of me sitting in front of Father on his hunter Ariel in 1941 just before he was posted abroad. While he was away he exhorted my mother to teach my brother and me to ride. This nearly ended in disaster when with mother holding my brother Nigel in front of her on her horse, and me on a leading rein, we bolted and all fell. However, no lasting damage was done, but not much further riding took place before Father returned from the war.

He said in later years that he nearly did not start riding again but what got him going was to teach the family. It was thus that the horse, and in the Christmas holidays hunting, totally dominated our lives. We started with highland ponies, the original Polly and her son Glen, both splendid and reliable children's ponies. At the age of 12 I was put on a horse but nearly gave up riding, having been jumped off so often. An old horse dealer suggested a special pad attached to the front of the saddle over the knees might help, and with this I gradually became more secure.

While the Braes of Derwent was our nearest pack, most of our hunting in the late forties and early fifties was with the Zetland, where the joint master and huntsman, Colin MacAndrew, provided great sport. The Zetland hunted north and south of the Tees. Old Lord Barnard, who owned 60,000 acres in the heart of the country, was the other joint master and ensured that his estate was mostly grass with minimum wire. There was also good hunting country on the North Yorkshire side. In the mid fifties Father transferred his allegiance to George Fairbairn, Master of the Tynedale, another, at that time, mainly grass country. The Tynedale and Zetland were equidistant from home.

I was of course very spoilt so far as riding and hunting were concerned. Paddy Farrell, the head groom, assisted latterly by Tommy Greenlay, the coachman, looked after the horses. The brewery horsebox driver Alf Browne took the horses to the meet, and Gerry Knotley the butler cleaned the clothes. I hardly had to lift a finger.

Other activities included fishing where my father sometimes in the Easter holidays took a beat on the Tweed, but we never went abroad. In the summer we went to the beach at Marsden, South Shields, where Vaux had the 'Grotto', a pub in a former smugglers' cave, and also another beach at Seaburn by Sunderland where Vaux had a Swallow hotel. At both these beaches we were expected by Father to swim, always a bracing experience in the North Sea! I remember in about 1946 staying at Saltburn near Redcar with its water-powered beach cable cars. One not very happy time was when my parents decided to go to Devon, to a hotel at Saunton Sands. This was not deemed a success by my brother Nigel and me. We hated the long drive to get there and being so far from home.

With five sons my mother was overwhelmed by masculine company. Girls hardly featured until mid teens, when there were some parties in Northumberland. Sedate by modern standards they were wild for those days, memorable for one's first kiss but nothing much more, not even a grope!

When not hunting or shooting it was riding that was the main activity. We moved to Southill in 1954 after my grandfather died and Father had the whole estate made so we could ride and jump anywhere. This we did wearing only a cloth cap. It was considered a bit 'prissy' to wear a hard hat in those days. It was during this time that the sport of 'eventing' was becoming increasingly popular. Eventing consists of Dressage, Cross Country and Show Jumping. It was a sport that apart from the dressage, exactly fitted. Before leaving Harrow I was to ride in my first 'event' and this was to lead on for the following 10 years or so to a consuming activity extending to point-to-pointing and then steeplechasing.

All in all holidays were very special. Father always somehow managed to take time off for riding, hunting and shooting with us. Mother rode in the early days sidesaddle, but after a nasty fall, she did not participate thereafter. She was always there however, moderating Father's sometimes excessive keenness and expectations, but she had three small sons to look after – Andrew, born in '45, Mark in '50 and Frank in '54, so she had her hands full with a young family in spite of a series of nannies and au pairs. She had also a big house to run, and although it had a full staff of butler, cook, gardeners and dailies, it was a major management task in itself to ensure it ran smoothly, as it always did.

From the time he came back from the war my father was always keen to involve me in Vaux Breweries. My grandfather had died on 28th December 1952, having a big funeral in the Cathedral on the last day of that year. He had nominally been Chairman until his death, but following the death of my grandmother in 1948, had played little part in the brewery. While I think Father hoped that one or more of his sons would follow him into the brewery, he made it clear that any son wishing to come in would have to be qualified in a profession first.

I was always highly aware of Vaux. Travelling around the North East, the name and the distinguishing V sign above the doors of hundreds of pubs all through the region gave me a pride from an early age that it was my grandfather Sir Frank and my father who were responsible.

Usually several times every holiday, my father took me to the Brewery where I could immerse myself in the mysteries of brewing under the watchful eyes of a succession of Head Brewers, particularly Mr Norman Curry and after him Doctor Bennison. I would sample the product in the form of a 'shandy', after the beer was diluted by a lemonade also made at the Brewery. I came to know many of the families who had been with the brewery almost from the beginning such as the Wrights and the Carters, who in their own way were as much part of the Vaux story as the Nicholsons. I was particularly excited by the stables where some 30 Percheron heavy horses, alongside some lighter horses who doubled as coach horses, delivered the beer to all the pubs within a five-mile radius of Sunderland. In the days of acute fuel rationing, this was an important saving. Red and Gold were the company colours used everywhere from the outside of the pubs to the wagons and on most of the promotional material.

When I was a teenager, my father took me along as a witness to some fraught negotiations to buy Workington Brewery as he sought to strengthen Vaux's presence in the North West where he had acquired in the late 1940s the Whitwell Mark Company in Kendal. His attempt was frustrated when Workington's Directors distributed sufficient shares to their friends to make it impossible for Vaux to buy the majority. This was legal at the time and of course long before there was a takeover panel.

I don't think I was totally brainwashed with the idea of going into Vaux, but my school holidays did instil a love of the North East which has never left me. Sons of dominant fathers often have a desire to outperform their parents. I was no different and I guess that by the time I left school, I had mapped out in my own mind what I wanted to do after National Service and Cambridge. I agreed with the idea of becoming an accountant, then I certainly hoped to join Vaux although, as I explain later, when the time came after a successful spell qualifying in accountancy, I was more than a little tempted to pursue a career in that profession and in the City.

CHAPTER 2

Young Adult

ON 14TH SEPTEMBER 1956, most of the 80 or so recruits arriving at The Guards Depot, Caterham were having their first experience of the adult world. There were a few who had been to university first and were thus more mature, but the majority, probably some 90%, of the intake to the Sept. '56 Brigade Squad were fresh from public schools.

Brigade Squads were the basic training units for potential officers of the Household Division of the army. The Household Division consisted of two cavalry regiments who formed the Household Cavalry and five regiments of foot guards collectively known as the Brigade of Guards. In history regiments of the Household Division had special responsibility for guarding the Monarch. They are still the only regiments who take part in the annual Queen's Birthday Parade on Horseguards in Whitehall.

Members of the Household Division considered themselves something of an elite, but whether they were regarded as such by others is open to question. The basic training, particularly for officers, was probably tougher than the norm, although not as tough as for some other parts of the armed forces such as the Royal Marines.

Even in 1956 there was some controversy about the Household Division's policy of separating potential officers from the rest. It didn't happen in other regiments where recruits from whatever walk of life did their basic training together. The Division's response was, they believed it was necessary to put potential officers through a much tougher regime than ordinary recruits. This had its advantages, but did mean that those of us who went this route never experienced at first hand how our men thought and lived.

We quickly realized just how tough it was. Immediately upon arrival we were chased at the double to our quarters where a 'trained soldier' was in charge of each barrack hut. He was responsible for enforcing discipline. The Coldstream Guards contingent of twenty-one recruits occupied one of the four 'Brigade Squad' Nissen huts. The regime consisted initially of drill, spit and polish, then more drill. Conversation with colleagues was only allowed during infrequent Naafi breaks. The regime was probably harsher then most prisons. I see from letters home that we considered our trained soldier particularly sadistic in his enjoyment of trashing recently bulled up boots and kit so that cleaning had to start all over again. Whenever we spoke to a trained soldier we had to stand to attention and address him by his rank up to sergeant – above that they were all 'Sir'. After four weeks we passed off the square. Thereafter the regime was slightly relaxed. Drill was interspersed with more varied military training such as basic weapon handling and tactics.

Of course twenty-one fit young men flung together talked when allowed, mainly about the opposite sex. Those of us (the majority) who were innocents, listened enthralled to claimed sexual conquests boasted of by some of the rest. Our basic training was due to take some 12 weeks during which time we took the selection exam for officers (known as WOSBIE). It was very necessary to pass, and not all did. When the time came there were a number who were either put back or failed. Their fate was then indeed to learn about the other side of life as ordinary guardsmen. During our time at Caterham we were virtually shaven headed, and I particularly recall the medical parade where we were given our jabs (injections). The medical officer came down the line of bared arms using the same needle, hardly wiping it in between. When one of the company, a strapping rugby forward, collapsed in a faint, the MO merely bent down and jabbed him on the ground. Of the twenty-one Coldstream recruits we knew the regiment had officer vacancies for less than half. While a few had failed WOSBIE it remained a very competitive world when we marched away some 12 weeks later, en route to Eaton Hall Officer Cadet School.

Eaton Hall in early 1957 had been since the war an officer training school, mainly for the infantry. It was originally the home of the Duke of Westminster. The hall itself, subsequently demolished, was a Victorian building built by the same architect who built St Pancras Station and in similar style. From what I remember, it was actually used mainly for offices and for some catering. We Officer Cadets lived in Nissen huts in the grounds. Still hanging on the walls of the main house were many of the ducal picture treasures, the most prominent being Rubens' 'Adoration of the Magi' – possibly one of the greatest religious paintings on earth, but not treated with much respect. It was not unknown, after a passing out dinner, for the picture to be the target of the odd missile, such as a tomato.

We were there to learn how to be infantry officers. We continued to have the inevitable drill, although on a considerably less arduous basis than at Caterham, and we were taught basic military tactics. A week or so was spent at a Battle Training Camp in the Welsh Mountains. The Coldstream contingent were part of a platoon commanded by a parachute officer. The company sergeant major (CSM) was a delightful Irish Guardsman. We were allowed cars and I had an old Austin of 1950 vintage. I was very fortunate, in that one evening we had been invited to the Liverpool Old Coldstream Association dinner and I was giving a lift to the CSM, when I was caught speeding. The CSM undoubtedly felt guilty about this and to be in his good books was well worth the £3 fine eventually meted out by the local bench.

My parents had a number of friends and acquaintances living close by who kindly asked me over. They included Sir Watkin and Lady Williams Wynn. He was a former Japanese prisoner of war and a major landowner. He was somewhat dour of disposition, but his wife Jean was lovely and very kind, sadly she was to die relatively young of cancer. I also was asked out by George Ridley the agent to the Westminster Estates. He was reputed to have started life sweeping the leaves of the drive at Eaton Hall but his great talents had been recognized by the 2nd Duke the famous Bendor and Ridley was largely responsible for protecting the huge

Grosvenor fortune through the days of penal taxation and death duties. In the late forties he had bought for the Duke almost every bit of agricultural land available in Britain as this attracted death duty relief. He also developed the enormous Westminster holdings on the West coast of Canada. He told the story of how he had, while in Canada, once received by telegram an immediate summons from the Duke to come back. Using train and stratocruiser as the fastest means of travel, he had arrived back after a fraught journey of several days at the Duke's Irish abode to be greeted by the Duke with 'Ridley, the logs are damp.' This was the only reason for the summons back!

Among the estates the Duke had bought in 1946 was the Brancepeth Estate where we remained tenants of my birthplace Quarry Hill under an agriculture protected lease after my parents moved to my grandfather's house.

With less than half likely to make the regiment Eaton Hall was even more competitive than Caterham. The decision was going to rest with the Coldstream officer stationed at Eaton Hall, the Assistant Adjutant Peter Egerton Warburton. Somehow I was one of the nine who made it.

While there were three of these who had strong family connections with the regiment, there were some surprise choices among the rest. Among the rejects were several who subsequently have had distinguished careers.

Those of us who had been fortunate enough to make the cut were despatched in April 1957 to one of the three battalions the regiment then had. The first and third battalions were based in Germany, while the second was performing 'public duties' in London which primarily involved guarding the Royal Palaces. I and three others were sent to the third battalion based near Dusseldorf. Life as a young Brigade of Guards officer was very pleasant. We had, I am afraid, an exaggerated idea of our own importance and standing. Each of us was allocated a soldier servant, whose main duty was to see we were immaculately turned out. There was not a great deal to do, there were of course the inevitable parades and we were each allocated a platoon consisting of a sergeant, 3 lance corporals, and some 25 guardsmen which we were expected to train and lead on regimental parades or exercises. There was plenty of time for polo. There was a tradition in the regiment not to be terribly welcoming to young officers initially, until they had found their feet. Other traditions included not removing hats in the mess. I remember entering the mess for breakfast the first day, and saying Good Morning to a colleague sitting behind his newspaper, to be firmly told officers in the regiment did not say Good Morning to each other!

The summer of 1957 passed very pleasantly. I was allowed three days leave to watch my brother Nigel play cricket at Lords, in the Eton and Harrow match, otherwise there were parties and 'mess nights', which were formal officer dinners with regular officers wearing evening 'mess dress'. We national service officers wore a smart blue uniform. There was also polo. The regiment owned some ponies, which made the game for the only time in my life affordable.

That autumn I was posted back to the Pirbright training area where I was put in charge of the regiment's boy soldiers. These consisted of some 30 boys aged 16 to 17½, destined mainly for the band. I am afraid I found my time there frustrating and boring. I got on the wrong side of the 'Adjutant', who was the officer responsible for discipline. For some petty reason, he awarded me a number of extra picquet duties, and also made me spend Christmas more or less on my own, as officer in charge of a Scarborough training camp. It was fortunate for me that the organization of the boys changed, making my job redundant, so that I could be sent back to Germany for the spring and summer of 1958. I was allowed leave to ride in my first 3-day event at Badminton, otherwise, like the previous summer, there was polo and parties. There were one or two wild nights in dubious places in Dusseldorf where a number of us lost our 'innocence'.

I had a car, which enabled me to go with brother officers on trips to Baden Baden and Heidelberg. The Nuburgring motor racing track was not far away, and I was there when the famous British driver Peter Collins was killed. Thanks to a £250 a year allowance from Father on top of my similar level of pay, I had enough money without being able to be extravagant.

We had very little contact with Germans. Many of the senior officers had served in the war, and had an inbuilt dislike of 'Krauts' and an attitude of no fraternization. There were one or two officers who befriended Germans, and I made a desultory effort to learn German, which really got nowhere, but overall we very much kept things within the Battalion. We hardly ever mixed, even with the Grenadier Guards next door.

We had a strict dress code, when not in uniform. For instance if we were in London none of us would be seen dead without a bowler hat, rolled umbrella and stiff white collar. We could walk past sentries, then outside the palace, tap twice with our umbrella and be saluted by the sentry. We had a special blazer known as a 'Guards Boating Jacket'. The Coldstream version has the regimental buttons in pairs as they are on dress uniform.

Mess life in Germany was pleasant, the size of one's mess bill very much depended on success or otherwise at cards. I had a tremendous run of beginner's luck when introduced to poker and complacently thought that this was the easy way to live. Latterly my luck changed with a vengeance, but fortunately I had not squandered my original winnings. Drink was duty free and plentiful and one had to learn to hold it. There were the occasional nights when I found my head spinning on laying it on the pillow. Fortunately I somehow bluffed through at next morning's parade.

Of my contemporaries a few have remained close friends, among them particularly John Pilley, who started army life in the next door bed to me. He was the only one in our hut who had been to University before National Service, and thus was somewhat more mature than the rest of us. John stayed on in the regiment as a regular soldier for some years before going into the city. There he still looks after the investments of a prominent and respectable Saudi family. Others I am always pleased to see when I go sometimes to the annual dinner of the regimental dining club for Coldstream Officers, the 'Nulli Secundus Club', known in the regiment as 'The Nulli'. The Coldstream Guards were officially the second senior guards regiment to the Grenadier Guards. However we had been raised as a regiment by General Monk in 1660 when he marched south from Coldstream to restore King Charles II. While the king gave precedence to his own Grenadiers, we considered ourselves 'second to none'. In historic formations the Grenadiers formed the right of the line and the Coldstream the left.

In 1957 National Service was wound down, so the 1958 undergraduate intake at Cambridge had a higher proportion of 18 years olds than in previous years where most did National Service before University. Thus I went up to Cambridge at the same time as my brother Nigel. We were both at Clare College and were part of the last intake selected by the old Master, Sir Henry Thirkill. Each of the Cambridge colleges was and I believe still is, responsible for its own admissions and who it selects. Clare was to see a radical change in selection criteria. To have a family connection with the college became a negative. The 1958 and earlier intakes therefore had little in common with subsequent years. I don't believe however that the new policy made any material difference to the overall results.

University life is about making friends, developing one's intellect and views, and yes – having fun! The university was still, in those days, very male orientated. Most of us had little interaction with girls from the two ladies' colleges Girton and Newnham. All the other colleges were exclusively male. There were one or two girls who broke the mould. There was Princess Elizabeth of Toro – a beautiful girl from a kingdom in Uganda – she subsequently became Foreign Minister for that country, but rebuffed amorous advances by Idi Amin, and collected a large libel award when the *Mirror*, I think it was, published false allegations by Amin that she had had sex in a lavatory at Orly airport. Another highly social and beautiful girl was Judy Innes whose brother was at Clare. She became a successful journalist but subsequently featured in the gossip columns after an affair with the infamous Lord Kagan, possibly the only life peer before Lord Archer to have been a 'guest of her majesty', the euphemism for a gaol sentence. I only ever once visited Girton to advise a horsey lady about stabling.

I read economics in my first year which I did not much enjoy. I then read law where I fared somewhat better. The prime means of teaching was through lectures. These were reinforced by 'tutorials' within each college where groups of two or three met a tutor once a week to present and discuss essays. Our law tutor was Keith, later Lord, Wedderburn. While he was a friendly man, he did not really approve of people from a public school background. We used rather deliberately to incite him by prejudiced remarks. His left wing instincts made him wince at some of our attitudes, and at one particular tutorial, where we had goaded him more than was fair, he left the room and wasn't seen again for some months. I hope the nervous collapse the poor man suffered was nothing to do with his visible upset at our attitudes!

Friends at University are often friends for life. Unfortunately my greatest friend Michael Allhusen was killed in a car crash, but there were others who have played a part in my life. Among the more remarkable is Gilbert Hinkley OBE, son of a Sheffield steel magnate. He is now very high up in the St John's Order, with the title of 'Hospitaller'. His main activity then was chasing, with so he alleged success, any nubile being in a skirt. He became a highly successful businessman who has made a great contribution in Derbyshire. Another at Clare who remains a close friend is Peter Vey. He had a sad first marriage to a lovely girl, where their two children died under 10 from a genetic disorder. However, as a mature father he now has three young sons with his second wife.

Cambridge has a long four month summer vacation from early June until October. The first of these I spent in France, in theory to learn French, at a summer school, but in practice there were too many Scandinavian beauties among fellow students with a relaxed outlook to life, and a desire to practise their English, so progress was not great. The second summer vacation was much more exciting. My Father had grown up with Tom de Pledge, son of the vicar of Sunderland who inherited from an uncle a quarter of a million-acre property on the North West coast of Australia. There I went as a 'Jackaroo' mustering cattle and sheep mainly on horseback. The plane to Australia in those days made frequent stops, Rome – Cairo – Teheran – Bombay – Calcutta – Singapore – Darwin. I had a short break in Singapore, staying at Raffles Hotel in great luxury and entertained by another old friend of my father, the general in charge of the garrison, General (later Field Marshall) Sir Richard Hull. I had bought from Simpson's in Piccadilly a special white tropical suit for the occasion, which turned out to be very out of place.

After the luxury of the Raffles Hotel I flew next day, changing planes at Darwin, to Derby on the North West coast of Australia to stay at the Grand Hotel. This was a 'dead ringer' for the pub in the film *Crocodile Dundee* with no hot water and with dormitory beds. What a contrast! From Derby, I caught the weekly mail plane, a DC3 already some 15 years old, which flew round the cattle stations. My destination, Mandora, was on the coast between Port Hedland (160 miles south) and Broome (230 miles north). The nearest neighbours were some 60 miles away on either side, while behind us was some 1,000 miles or more of desert. My host Tom de Pledge and his wife were in their mid fifties. He had a prodigious, and in the end, life destroying thirst, consuming around two bottles of gin or whisky each day. Nevertheless they were extremely kind to the rather gauche young man who descended on them. They had two children, Didy, a very pretty girl whom I had met in England and took to a May Ball at Cambridge before I came out, and Joey, the son and heir, who still owns the property. The station was then mainly a mixed cattle and sheep station.

Apart from one white overseer, the 'boys' who mustered the cattle and sheep were all aborigines, jolly people of charm, but not of high productivity. They were treated rather as children, even pets, with given names such as 'Monkey' who had a wife 'Peanut'. Station owners were far from politically correct by today's standards! However the 'boys' were excellent stockmen, and their wives, including a wonderful old camp cook 'Maud', who looked after us when we were in the bush, were considerable characters. They seemed happy and probably were much more so than their descendants who, in that part of the world, no longer work on Stations. They apparently mostly fritter away their time on reservations, often seriously the worse for alcohol. Going back, as I did in 1999, nearly 40 years later, it was sad to see the lack of dignity among the few aborigines I saw, compared to 1960.

On the station I spent blissful and happy days on horseback and camping in the bush, although on beds because of the fear of Deaf Adder snakes, reputed to be lethal. I only ever saw one of these dead, having been run over, but I did see plenty of Red Back Spiders which are highly poisonous. A favourite place for them around the homestead was the loo, a tin shack at the end of the garden with a corrugated roof. Gentlemen and indeed ladies were well advised to lift the seat, and check before doing their business.

I was there midwinter, with a day time temperature up to the eighties, but cooler at nights, although we all slept on the veranda when in the homestead. In their summer it must be really unbearably hot and sticky and also subject every few years to hurricanes.

While there, my host arranged for me to go to Broome, then a great pearling centre, and also to a legendary cattle station in the Kimberleys – Fossil Down. It was over 1 million acres (1500 square miles). The homestead, unlike Mandora which was basically a series of tin shacks, was built of granite in a Spanish style. The property belonged to Bill MacDonald, whose grandfather had driven the cattle up some 2,000 miles from New South Wales during the 1880s. He and his wife Maxine maintained an elegant lifestyle. Their daughter, Merrily, was the head stockman, a stunningly beautiful girl, who unfortunately for me showed little interest in a visiting English boy! She was devoted to her job and lived for horses and cattle. It was 'Wild West' country and the MacDonalds were reputed to be virtually at war with their neighbours, with tales of gunfire, and cattle raiding. The Kimberleys themselves contain some spectacular scenery which consisted of large plains with great granite ranges running across.

Back at Mandora it was horse-mustering time. In those days the horse was the main means of rounding up the cattle – now it is motorbikes and even light planes. The horses ran more or less wild, but every year were rounded up for branding and gelding, a rather brutal process. Those required as stock horses were broken to saddle and the rest released. The quality of horses was quite good as thoroughbred stallions were mostly used, although the occasional 'Brumbie' was not caught up in time, and became a wild stallion of mixed blood.

At the end of my six weeks at Mandora I was due to fly to Perth, but my host decided he needed to drive and would take me on the 1,400 mile drive south as he wanted to change his pick-up. We set off on dirt roads over the first 800 miles, stopping off at various cattle stations on the way. My host who was driving would yell 'snort' every hour or so, whereupon it was my job to replenish his whisky glass. In 1960 the breathalyser had not been heard of! But in any case the road was more or less dead straight, and one only probably saw half a dozen other vehicles all day, until getting closer to civilization.

Perth where we were headed is the capital of Western Australia. While it was, and is a beautiful city, it was regarded by the frontiersmen as almost the centre of the universe! Few ever visited the Australian east coast with its larger cities of Sydney and Melbourne. So far as West Australians were concerned, they felt no need to go further afield. They certainly had a point.

I however, after a few days in Perth, bade farewell to my host and went on to stay with cousins of his near Melbourne, then with the Hordens, a big ranching family in New South Wales, finishing with two weeks on a Queensland cattle station, another million acre property, but with entirely white stockmen. Their idea of a break was to put down their money in the local bar and stay and drink until the landlord told them there was no change left. A cynic commented that they rode their horses in the bar and their women (Sheilas) in the bush.

I came back from Australia seriously thinking that a life as a Jackaroo, and hopefully then a station owner, was the one for me.

1960, Cambridge University Drag Hounds, PDN on white horse, (L-R) Anthony Pemberton, Viscount Ullswater and Julian Courtauld.

It remained a romantic dream, only dispelled in 1999, when I went back to Mandora and realized what a hard life it actually was. Joe de Pledge, who now owns the station having inherited it from his father, has once been to England. Didy his sister married a Scotsman David Menzies of Menzies whom she met when he was ADC to the Governor of Western Australia. Sadly the marriage didn't work out because he wanted to live in Australia and she in Britain, and she now lives in London with her second husband. She still goes to visit her brother at Mandora, but there can hardly be a greater contrast between his life and hers.

Back at Cambridge for my final year, I became joint master of the Cambridge University Drag Hunt. I paid rather more attention to this than to my studies. It was a traumatic time. One morning a hound had gone missing and my joint master and I discussed who should go and look for it. He volunteered to go as I had an essay to complete. The next I knew was his parents arriving at my digs to tell me he had had an accident and did I know what he was doing. He died that night. Michael Allhusen was my greatest friend at Cambridge. It is a terrible, but all too common tragedy for a young man to be killed in a car accident. It happened on a straight piece of road in the morning. The theory was he may have sighted the hound and been distracted, but his car hit a telegraph pole. His parents asked me to do the identification and inquest which in itself was stressful, but something I felt privileged to do for them.

I have some happier memories of that year. One was being shown around the House of Lords and entertained to lunch by one of my predecessors as Lord Lieutenant, Lord Lawson of Beamish. Jack Lawson was one of ten children of a mining family. He had risen in miners' union and Labour party politics between the wars and had become a minister in Attlee's 1945 Government. When the Patrician 7th Marquess of Londonderry died in 1949, Clement Attlee the Prime Minister who had previously ennobled Lawson, appointed him Lord Lieutenant, a position he filled with distinction until 1958. He was not much over five feet tall but a great character. My father and he had become friends hence the invitation to the Lords where I was introduced on Christian name terms to everyone from the doorman to Monty. It was an awesome experience for a 23 year old. I did get to know around the same time another similar friend of my father, Sam Watson the great Durham Miners' leader of the sixties. He was totally at odds with the left wing elements of the miners' union, I remember him warning my father during Vaux's industrial troubles of 1965, that the 'Reds were not just under the bed, they were in the bed'.

When I started my final term at Cambridge, I found that I could not revise without provoking a severe headache, diagnosed as delayed concussion from a nasty fall I had had in a point to point during the Easter break. I was told I must not think or drink for two months, which conveniently covered my final exams. Cambridge has a rule that if unfit to take 'finals' an undergraduate can still be awarded an honours degree provided his tutors are satisfied that he would have passed if he had been well. I was fortunate that my tutor was prepared to oblige and I could get a degree classed as an 'Aegrotat' from the Latin verb for sickness. The only problem was that to qualify I had to keep the term by staying in Cambridge. It was a boring time as all my friends were frantically revising and didn't at all want to see me. Time hung heavily upon my hands. While I was quite happy not to 'think', not to 'drink' was harder! My lapses were in that department, rather than that of thought!

CHAPTER 3

The World of Work

I LEFT CAMBRIDGE in 1961 with my Bachelor of Arts (BA) degree. Converting a Cambridge BA into a Masters degree (MA) is a simple process. A graduate has merely to wait three years then pay five guineas. A number of BAs never bothered, knowing that if they wanted to they always could. A rumour went round in the mid sixties that the system however was to change and that to obtain an MA would in future require further study, as it does in probably every other university in the world outside 'Oxbridge'. Thus a number of us duly turned up for a ceremony and party and became Cambridge MAs. The rumour however was false and to this day the system remains the same.

Leaving Cambridge was not the end of my education. In America qualifications in such as law, medicine, architecture or as in my case in accountancy are usually in the shape of Masters degrees or Doctorates. Therefore it is not unusual to remain in full time education until aged in the late 20s. In Britain while we leave University and the official education scene, we still have to study to obtain our formal qualifications. I was to study to become a Chartered Accountant, the requirements for which in 1961 were to serve three years 'articles' as an apprentice to a partner. An 'articled clerk' had to pass intermediate and final exams which were far from a push over. They required intense study outside working time.

For the princely stipend of £156 per year I started my 'articles' in September 1961. I was an apprentice to Michael Coates who had connections with the North East but was soon to become senior partner of Price Waterhouse. They were the Vaux Auditors. Michael was the son of a legendary North East character – 'JMS' Coates, who had established himself as the trustee of most of the great estates and families of the North East. At the time I joined, 'JMS' still had an office with the firm in Newcastle, where I was initially based.

This meant living with my parents in considerable comfort and enjoying all the amenities, in particular the horses. I didn't find it too difficult to study in the evenings mainly by correspondence course, but it did mean frequently burning the midnight oil. As a result when the first exam results were announced, I had achieved honours, passing in the top 1%. This gave me considerable credibility with my employers, who fortunately took an indulgent and friendly attitude to my horse oriented extracurricular activities. I don't know of any other articled clerk who rode in the Grand National while serving his time.

After I passed my intermediate exam I was based in Price Waterhouse's London office. I was tempted to remain in the profession, as by the time I passed my finals, I was earning £1,200 per year and was among the highest paid articled clerks in the country. However I decided that at the age of twenty six I would rather be in general management and I had a unique opportunity.

Even in the sixties, there would be some raised eyebrows at the idea of a son joining as an executive of a public company where his father was Chairman. In my case however, I had earned my spurs as an accountant, I was a highly marketable commodity and could easily have stayed in the city or gone elsewhere.

I thought hard about whether I was wise to come back. I was sensitive to my position as Chairman's son, while the fashionable view then was that Vaux would not long survive before it was taken over. Many similar sized Brewery companies had disappeared in the late fifties and early sixties but these were mainly family owned companies where the family found the temptation of money in the bank too hard to resist. Vaux, although perceived as a family company, was not, and this in theory made it even more vulnerable.

However what drew me back more than any other factor was that even as a boy, Vaux had been so much part of my life. I had enormous respect for my father. He was not prepared to take in sons who were not qualified in their own right in a profession, but as I had more than met his expectations in this regard, he would have been bitterly disappointed had I turned down the opportunity he was offering and I believed that we could and would survive and continue to maintain a proud place, creating employment and serving our customers in the North East and further afield.

I had trained as an accountant because at the time it was the best available business training. There were no business schools as such in the UK. Harvard Business School in America was well established but only a very few of my generation from the UK went there.

An over-emphasis on accountancy can be counter-productive and accountants are sometimes rightly accused of an inability to see the big picture. However, what the training does teach, is the importance of thoroughness and attention to detail. It does not of itself teach management skills, or leadership, which is hard to define in a textbook but comes more from genes and upbringing.

I joined Vaux and Associated Breweries Ltd at the beginning of 1965 as assistant to the managing director – my father who was also the chairman – a position he had held since the death of my grandfather 13 years earlier. Vaux in the fifties and early sixties had expanded in Scotland, buying two breweries in Edinburgh and a third in Perth. While Sunderland remained the headquarters of Vaux, the company was facing in the North East serious problems of a declining customer base because of the contraction of the coalmining and shipbuilding industries. The brewing industry itself was undergoing major consolidation, largely under the influence of the Canadian E.P. Taylor. He built the first major brewing conglomerate acquiring and merging a number of family companies, such as Hope and Anchor and Hammonds in Yorkshire, and Tennants in Scotland, into United Breweries. He then merged with Charrington, at the time a major London brewer, and subsequently with Bass, Mitchells and Butler to form the UK's largest brewer. He had approached Vaux but was politely rebuffed. Following on from Taylor's activities came the tripartite merger to form Allied Breweries, of Ind Coope, a national brewer based in Burton-on-Trent but trading mainly in the South, Ansells based in Birmingham and Tetleys the leading Yorkshire brewery.

During the fifties Vaux had held discussions with Newcastle Breweries, particularly with Edward Reid, my father's closest industry friend. He died prematurely in the late fifties and Newcastle Breweries was acquired instead by Scottish Brewers, itself an amalgamation of McEwans Brewery and two Younger breweries. After Edward Reid died, his successor, Col James Porter was reputed in my family to have fled to Scottish Brewers in fear that otherwise Vaux would acquire them. My Father and Col Porter did not get on.

In the early stages, the acquisitions and mergers were friendly. The hostile take-over only became a feature of brewing corporate life in the late fifties, with Charles Clore's unsuccessful bid for Watneys. By the time I joined Vaux it was a hot subject of speculation as a potential target for a hostile bid. This situation was never to change throughout my 34 years with the company. This was a considerable spur to achievement.

The 1960s particularly following the Labour government election in 1964 established a trend which was to last until 1979 towards growing employee militancy and trade union power. Vaux, which had set up employee consultative committees in the fifties, was not unionized in Sunderland, although the Scottish end was. However during 1964 and 1965 many of the employees did join the Transport and General Workers Union, but the majority did not. The general atmosphere on the shop floor in Sunderland became tense between union and non-union employees, and even more so in Scotland where the union organizer was a typical militant of that era. This was to lead at the end of my first year in the company, to a 'work to rule' by a majority of transport drivers in the run up to Christmas. It was because of this, that in a move celebrated at the time, my father stood on a wagon on New Years Eve and sacked some sixty drivers who had earlier brought back undelivered loads and had, on being questioned, stated that they were working to rule.

There appeared to be three ringleaders of the action. Two of these were local but the real leader was a man who disappeared quickly after the blow up. There was evidence subsequently that he was a professional troublemaker insinuated into the company by one of the Trotskyist fringe groups who created so much mayhem throughout industry in the sixties and seventies.

After the New Year break we recruited, without much difficulty, replacement drivers, but attempts were made to close down the company by picketing deliveries of supplies, particularly oil. Vaux had to buy an oil tanker which initially collected oil from local sources. It was driven very courageously by Alf Browne who normally drove the horses. While he had a member of management beside him when driving through pickets, it was a major ordeal for him, but he was an outstanding driver thoroughly committed to the company and its principles of fairness. When this tanker was 'blacked', we had to buy a second tanker which the pickets never knew of. The procedure was for the blacked tanker to leave Sunderland and drive to my father's farm where the second tanker would transfer the oil. The pursuing pickets were stopped by police at the gates of the farm and never discovered what was happening. Slowly the situation eased, an eventual compromise was reached, allowing a handful of those dismissed to be reinstated.

It was unusual at the time for a company to be able to win such a confrontation. This was only possible because a substantial number of Vaux drivers were prepared to defy pickets and remained loyal to the company. We were saved by the tradition of fair treatment and mutual respect which had been developed in the company and which remained a major feature of the corporate culture until betrayed in 1999.

I learnt a lot about industrial relations during this time, particularly about the need to be firm but fair. As a result, the company never again had a major industrial relations problem, although in Scotland there were minor problems, culminating in certain militant activists contaminating a batch of beer. While we could not prove who the culprits were, we dismissed two we knew were responsible, and there was no reaction from the remaining workforce who, like us, knew we had sacked the right people.

While my baptism of fire was in industrial relations, I did spend time in every section of the brewery, and visited each of the 600 pubs we then owned. I also spent a short time with Courage Brewery in London and Ushers of Trowbridge in Wiltshire, learning about the perspectives of big companies or subsidiaries of big companies in the industry.

Vaux had opened its first substantial Swallow Hotel – the Golden Circle at Bathgate, in the early sixties and in 1968 a well known former Tory politician, Robert Boothby, opened for us the rebuilt Bellahouston Hotel in Glasgow, making in his speech rather unfortunate comments about decadent family dynasties! Swallow Hotels otherwise then consisted mostly of a collection of country inns built up in the fifties. They were considered excellent at the time although few of them boasted 'en suite' facilities. To go for a bath or to the loo, often involved a trip down the passageway even in four star establishments. I quickly foresaw development of hotels as an area of growth for the company, but in my early years with the group my father needed some convincing. It was not until 1972 that I finally persuaded him to form Swallow as a separate division of the group, combining the English and Scottish Hotels. After this Vaux's hotel business really began to develop.

When I joined the Company the Vaux Board was, in some ways, ahead of its time. Apart from my father, all the other directors were non executive, two of them had been inherited from pre war acquisitions but the other three, while from allied trades to the company – malting, sugar and wine – were 'independent' although these possibly would be criticized in the current climate as being selected by the Chairman.

Having spent my first year going round the business, I was fortunate to be sent on a marketing course at Harvard, organized by the International Marketing Institute. It consisted of six weeks in the business school being taught by the famous Harvard case study method, then a six week study tour of America through the midwest to San Francisco and back through Washington.

On the course were students from a number of countries including Czechoslovakia behind the Iron Curtain. That country was then enjoying a liberalization of the regime leading up to 'the Prague Spring' of 1968, which was of course then brutally suppressed by Soviet tanks. One of the others on the course was a lively Afghani called Ahmad Mousa. Ahmad was more interested in the local female talent than his studies. Many years later in the early eighties I received a telephone call from Ahmad telling me he was in London and a refugee from Afghanistan. He went on 'I have no money'. Alarmed at this and expecting to be asked for a loan, I gingerly enquired what he really had. The reply was 'only three quarters of a million dollars'. At the time this was considerably more than I had! Anyhow Ahmad eventually settled I believe in Southern California and when I last heard of him he was doing well in property.

The Institute opened my eyes to the importance of marketing in selling products. However good the product may be, unless the potential customer both knows of its existence and is put in the mood to buy, the product be it goods or a services will not sell except as a 'commodity', where it is not likely to be very profitable.

Harvard uses the case study method of teaching. Small groups known as 'Can Groups' because in earlier times they were reputed to meet in communal lavatories, sit round and debate a 'case' consisting of a business situation and problem drawn from real life. A nominee of each group then presents its findings in a class session moderated by a Professor. It is a very effective means of education.

Harvard Business School sets a very demanding schedule of study and classes but it was summer, the weather was hot and sunny, and there was time for relaxation. There were some lovely girls attending summer courses at Radcliffe, the sister college of Harvard. I fell half in love with one of them, a very pretty girl, and I think she may have with me, but it was all very innocent. I am afraid when I left America, I rather brutally broke it up because I thought her background was so different from mine, and she wouldn't find England attractive. I never thought I would see her again so it was a considerable surprise to be told by a friend while out shooting, some 15 years later, that he had been asked by the wife of a high powered American banker, recently arrived in London, whether he knew 'Paul Nicholson'. Anyhow, she and her husband are good friends, although now they live back in America, we do not see much of them.

While on the study tour in San Francisco, I had an introduction to Fritz Maytag who was developing the first of the boutique American Breweries. He had bought, when he was a student at Stanford University, a run down tiny brewery in the heart of the city. He had then built an entirely new small brewery deliberately using an old technique of shallow vessels for fermenting the beer developed for brewing beer in a hot climate before the age of lagering and chilling. These vessels during the fermenting process, gave off a mist which looked like steam. Fritz's brewery was therefore known as the 'Anchor Steam' Brewery. It was at the time a cult beer but only sold in Northern California. It has developed nationwide since. Fritz has avoided the temptation to seek high volumes going rather for a high margin. While he has been much emulated, he is still the leader in the premium section of the ale market. Fritz also bought in the sixties, for a few thousand dollars only, the York Creek Vineyard in the hills above the Napa Valley. An investment the worth of which has multiplied many times.

The study tour moved on after California to Denver Colorado. Here we visited Coors Brewery. Coors' unique selling point at the time was that it cold filtered rather than pasteurized its products. It was a brand leader in the Western United States. Later it developed in the rest of the country where it has become the number three brewer in the United States. It has recently come over here buying brands which 'Interbrew' has been forced to dispose of by our UK competition authorities. The company is very much run by the Coors family with Pete Coors the current Chairman. Like Anheuser Busch, much of the marketing image, backed up by fact, is of quality products and not commodities.

At the end of the tour I spent some six weeks in New York

where I was with the Shaefer Brewery then based in the city, but now long gone. This was a commodity brewer. The most interesting experience I had with them was going around drinking dens in Harlem with some of their black salesmen. In spite of Harlem's reputation, I never felt any alarm. It was before drugs had taken a hold, and I did not see evidence of crime although there was a lot of poverty.

The American brewing industry was very different from ours in that since the repeal of prohibition, any form of 'tie' either of ownership or loan between a brewer and a retail outlet was forbidden. On the other hand, there were laws strictly regulating variations in terms of supply to different outlets so that such terms had to be open with no hidden forms of discount or backhander.

On my return from America I became a member of the Vaux board in 1967 at the age of 29. The profits of the Group had peaked in 1965. They then stagnated and only recovered in 1970. No dividend increase was paid for three years before then. The group was looking vulnerable. My father who had turned 60 in 1965 was still a formidable operator but his attention was focused increasingly on industry rather than Vaux matters, particularly following the reference of the industry to the Monopolies Commission in 1966 and his election as Chairman of the Brewers Society 1968-69, a position of which he was particularly proud, being the first son of a previous Chairman to be elected. He also had found a new sport in four-horse carriage driving, at which he excelled despite his age, going on to be a member of the winning British team in the first world championships in 1972, and coming third individually.

It was an uneasy time for me in the company. I had doubts whether I had been wise to join at all, and in a common situation in family-managed companies, I had a father who was reluctant to let go the reins. I was living at home, which while being very comfortable, was, with hindsight, a mistake, as it made it difficult to take actions with which he would not agree. I had been joined in the company by my third brother Andrew in 1969 and he was a good support, but it was really only after I moved away from the family home after my marriage in 1970, that I could begin to take the steps which would be necessary to secure another quarter century of successful existence for the Group.

Chapter 4

The Sporting Life

During the years 1958-1970, I was lucky to enjoy fast horses, fast cars and fast planes, if not fast women! I was very spoilt so far as horses were concerned. There were grooms to look after the horse and the saddlery, and a butler/valet to clean boots and wash breeches. The basis of my horse activities was fox-hunting and in the sixties I enjoyed some marvellous hunting in Leicestershire, Ireland and in the North. It is difficult to explain to those not brought up with hunting that its thrill is not the kill. This happens infrequently, although sufficiently often to be a relatively humane way of maintaining a natural balance, when compared with other alternatives. The real thrill is the adrenaline filled ride across country over hedge, ditch, rails and wall. Surtees described hunting through his character 'Jorrocks' as, 'it is like war but with only 10% of the danger'. At Cambridge I was Master of the University drag hounds and some say why can't drag hunting replace foxhunting? The answer is that drag hunting is very different. There is a certainty about the direction of the chase, an artificiality about the route and the obstacles, and no time for the 'coffee housing' and socializing on horseback, that is so much part of a day out foxhunting, which can last five hours or more.

Many of those seeking to outlaw hunting fail to understand the passion behind the beliefs of its supporters. A day's hunting is not just about the chase but about enjoying the countryside and the company with horsemen, followers on foot and in cars providing a social cohesion that has mystic and almost religious overtones. Readers of Siegfried Sassoon's *Memoirs of a Foxhunting Man* may get some of the flavour of this.

I have in my possession a rare print by the famous horse artist 'Snaffles'. The print, entitled 'That Far Away Echo', depicts men in the First World War trenches, which must have been as near to Hell on earth as it is possible to imagine. As in a dream the print depicts ghostly hounds and a huntsman blowing his horn. For such men this was their comfort and inspiration.

There is a real possibility that a ban on hunting will lead to a very different form of civil unrest than has happened before. Left or extreme right wing rioters are seeking to change the status quo. Countryside protesters are seeking to preserve the way of life they believe their fathers fought for.

As for the cruelty issue, a ban will lead to far greater suffering as foxes, which are basically pests, are shot and often wounded, or endure the agony of a snare. This is what is already happening in Scotland. There is no move, nor should there be, to outlaw Halal or Kosher killing. Any such attempt would be hugely provocative to our Muslim or Jewish minorities. But if the description of how these killings are carried out is correct then on any rational scale of cruelty these practices rank far higher than hunting. Even the best slaughterhouses, farms and fishing fleets involve a degree of fear, pain and suffering for animals. Those who enjoy the result of these processes, whether by eating fish, fowl or meat, or wearing leather shoes, could be accused of a degree of hypocrisy when seeking to outlaw hunting. Nature, of which mankind is a part, is 'red in tooth and claw'.

This is not to condone certain sadistic animal practices such as badger baiting or cock fighting, where the excitement is in the suffering. I personally find bullfighting rather repugnant, but I realize it has a similar mystic significance to millions of Hispanics as hunting has to its followers. Let us hope our liberal culture of tolerance and understanding will in the end prevail. The only country in the world that has laws banning foxhunting is Germany, and who brought these laws in? – the Nazi regime.

I played a part in other sports which spring from the chase, particularly Eventing, Point-to-Pointing and Steeplechasing. Eventing grew as a sport in Britain during the fifties. It consists of three phases – Dressage, riding Cross Country and Show Jumping. There are one day events where all three phases are compressed, with a Cross Country phase which is considerably less arduous than in the major events over three days held at Badminton and Burleigh, and in the early days at Harewood. Dressage consists of making the horse perform precise movements at walk, trot and canter, perfectly balanced at all times. In its highest form some of the movements are almost dancing, but for eventing purposes the movements are more practical. Riding Cross Country is against pre-set timings requiring a bold horse with a good gallop. To reach the top the horse needs to be a near thoroughbred. He must be able to jump precisely over a variety of obstacles including into and out of water. The Show Jumping requires accuracy so as not to dislodge poles and other obstacles which unlike Cross Country obstacles are not fixed solid. I rode in my first event in 1956, a one-day affair at Fenton in Northumberland. Army Training meant no time in 1957, but my father, for whom eventing was a natural extension of his horsemanship, rode at Badminton having won a one day event at Fenton in Northumberland that year.

In 1958 I obtained sufficient leave from the Army to ride not very successfully at Badminton where I did not complete the course. 1959 was the high point of my eventing career when I rode two horses at Badminton and two in the European championships at Harewood considered to be the biggest course seen up to that time. One fence, consisting of parallel poles, was so wide that my horse was able to jump into the middle, stop and come out at the side. As the flags were on the front, this did not count as a 'refusal' which would have meant taking the fence again, something I do not think I would have had the courage to do! However I did not manage to stay aboard so incurred the penalty for a fall. Father also rode two horses at Badminton that year and in October I was part of a British team in the French Championships at Fontainebleau. I didn't succeed in completing the course and that was my only international appearance.

When riding horses in races or endurance events, it is important to be as close as possible to the minimum stipulated weight. I am over 6ft 2 and not lightly built, so it was always a major struggle to bring my weight down. I reckon that over these years I became quite an expert on diet as well as a frequent visitor to the Newcastle Turkish baths with their naked masseurs, also to some less salubrious places in London and other parts of the kingdom. It probably was not good for health long term although I haven't yet suffered any serious ill effects. However three weeks before the French Championships at Fontainebleau I was struck down with painful shingles and the orthodox doctor said that it could take six weeks to recover. In some despair and in no way fit to ride, I went to see the most famous homeopath of his day Sir John Weir, who was by then in his eighties. He had treated generations of the royal family. The old man examined me, asking some strange questions about my beliefs and attitudes. He then went to his cupboard and brought out some jars of white powder, teaspoons of which he proceeded to place in a series of paper phials, which he instructed me to take in sequence. Three days later all signs of shingles had disappeared. I have tried homeopathic medicine since but never again with dramatic effects.

I last rode at Badminton in 1964. For three years before that I competed with an old school friend Patrick Conolly Carew. Neither of us were very good at Dressage and were near the bottom of the class at that stage of the competition, but did much better in the Cross Country phase. I gave up when Patrick suddenly became good at Dressage, but also because the sport was becoming increasingly professional, and while some participants were nice, there were many who thought themselves God's Gift to Horses.

I do have in my dressing room five plaques awarded to riders of horses who successfully complete Badminton. My father had won four plaques. If a competitor won five plaques he used to be awarded a silver 'armada' dish commemorating his achievement. My father was given a dish because one of my rides was credited to him. I never had the heart to point this out to him!

I was lucky enough to have one 'dream horse', but he was never going to be an eventer. Acquired as a 4-year-old in 1959, with the intention of being trained as an eventer, Sea Knight bucked me off the first time I rode him. In 1961 my brother Nigel who emigrated to Australia later that year, rode him in the Melton Cross Country race, run over four miles of natural Leicestershire country and finished well up. The next year, 1962, I won this race outright beating a field of 80 with many of the girls riding several stone lighter. I went on to win the Haydon and the Tynedale Open point to points and to be second in the 'Heart of all England', the North's premier novice hunter chase, and my first ride under National Hunt rules. 1963 was the year of the great frost lasting from early January until March. We had placed Sea Knight with the famous northern trainer Arthur Stephenson, a great character, and mentor to a number of leading amateur riders such as Chris Collins and Peter Greenall.

However, the great frost was a frustrating time. There was no question of racing, but I could not let up on my diet in case of a thaw. Because it would have interrupted the hunting season, I had never skied before. However the weather meant conditions were perfect in much of Scotland, and I and a lovely girlfriend joined a party that went first to watch the Scotland/Wales rugby match at Murrayfield, which had underturf heating and then went on up to ski at Glencoe. Neither of us had skied before but the others in the party included experts, particularly Daphne Arnott (later Scott Harden). Having hired our skis and gone up in the lift, my friend and I tried a few tentative moves, fell down and then held hands on the nursery slopes, while the others disappeared up the mountains. However our tryst was rudely interrupted by the sight of the 'bloodwagon' bearing poor Daphne who had had a cracking fall and had to be whisked off to hospital. It was enough to put me off skiing for another five years!

Eventually this frost thawed out and we were able to run Sea Knight at Newbury in early March. The objectives were the two 'Foxhunter' hunter chases at Cheltenham, then Liverpool. At Cheltenham, a four mile race, riding in my third race under rules I was at the back of the field much of the way. I then found in the last mile that I was overtaking horse after horse, finally being beaten a short head. Fortunately I learnt from my mistake next

1963, Painting by Tom Carr of Liverpool Foxhunters Race, PDN on No. 11 jumping Beechers Brook.

time out, notching up the first of my two victories over the National fences.

Winning the Foxhunters qualified me to ride in the Grand National in 1964. The preliminaries for this were not auspicious with a fall first time out that year and a third at Cheltenham. Sea Knight had been allocated 10 stone in the National handicap, a weight I could not possibly get down to. I went to a leading Harley Street dietician Dr Goller for advice on how to reduce my weight as far as possible. He put me on some pills and a diet consisting of only minimal food and four cups of liquid a day. I lived mainly on nicotine and caffeine. I had only taken up smoking aged 21 in 1959 as a hunger suppressant but like most in such a position became increasingly hooked, only finally giving up cigarettes on marriage in 1970.

I spent the day before the race in the Harrogate Turkish baths sweating out some 6lbs, so I actually weighed out at 10 stone 13lbs including saddle, but felt very weak.

I was always highly nervous before any race but it was

noticeable that before the National all the professionals were equally nervous, with recourse to nicotine being the main prop. The 1964 National was a cold day, and I had the thinnest of silk vests, barely decent white silk breeches and boots made of what felt like papier-mâché.

When we were called into line I was on the wide outside hoping to keep clear of trouble, and conscious that the main money on me was as the result of a local bookie offering 6-1 against 'getting round'. The field went off at a much faster pace than I was used to in hunter chasing and I was too weak to make Sea Knight keep up. However we did get round – fifteenth and last of the finishers out of a field of thirty one. My main memory is of gorging myself thereafter putting on over a stone in 24 hours.

Riding in the National is something I have dined out on ever since. When the subject of horses crops up, I can always get attention by casually stating 'I did get round the Grand National'! It was a never to be forgotten experience and the peak of my racing career, although there was a high point the following year, when I again won the Foxhunters, and in 1967 Sea Knight won a further five open point-to-points and I was first man beaten by two light weight women in the Melton race. Sea Knight was not my only point-to-point winner. In 1961 my brother won the Cambridge Undergraduates race at Cottenham with me second. I then won the next race, the 'Past and Present' on a borrowed horse. In 1965 my father bought for me a lovely point-to-pointer R.I.K. on which I won the Cheshire Forest Open point-to-point, two days before my big race, the Foxhunters. I also won the Zetland open race on him. Sadly I was riding R.I.K. when he broke a leg in a fall at Ayr. My final ride in a point-to-point was in 1970. My father had a horse called Pennylaw which I thought had potential but he didn't show it when ridden by other brothers. I volunteered to sweat down once again to ride 12 stone 7 in a maiden race and won that. After that, as I was engaged to a fiancée who was far from horsey, I hung up my racing boots, although I did go on hunting for a few years up until 1976.

Vaux were famous for their stables consisting of Percheron

1963, Mother leading PDN on Sea Knight after winning Foxhunters.

heavy horses and lighter carriage horses which as well as delivering beer were used for publicity and corporate hospitality purposes including pulling a coach. Encouraged by my father I learnt to drive a 4-in-hand in the early sixties taking part in my first coaching class at the 'Royal Show' in 1962 which that year was held in Newcastle. We have in our home a Tom Carr picture of all the family and company activities at that show consisting of two coaches, a 4-in-hand and pair of Percherons pulling Vaux carts, two show hunters, 2-in-hand Percherons, two Red Poll cows and a riding team consisting of Father, myself and Elaine Straker mother of the famous eventer Karen Dixon. Because I was new to 4-in-hand driving and a possible candidate for the prestigious Coaching Club the then President of the Club, Sir Dymoke White chose to ride with me. It was fortunate that he did. In the main ring my 'off wheeler' (right back) horse slipped and fell. We managed to stop while Sir Dymoke, by then well into his seventies, leapt off and organized grooms to sit on the horse's head while it was unhitched, so that it could get up none the worse for wear, to be rehitched, and carry on. My date sitting next to me was Annabel Legard who, while a fearless horsewoman in her own right, confessed to having been quite terrified. Touch wood! This has been my only real incident in 40 years of coaching, apart from hitting a bollard in Windsor while driving to Ascot in 1967. Surprisingly in the circumstances I was duly elected to the Coaching Club in 1965 although I did not do much driving until some 15 years later.

Most of my early social life revolved around horses. Great friends were the Carew family of Castletown outside Dublin. Pat the eldest was an exact contemporary at Harrow being one day older than me. His sister Diana was a hunting friend with whom I enjoyed a lot of fun going round hunting with various packs in Ireland. Lord and Lady Carew had brought up their family in Castletown, a huge Georgian mansion not in great repair. Lady Carew's mother was Lady Maitland, a Scottish heiress who lived at Thirlestane Castle in the Borders. As her son had been killed in the war, she strongly supported her daughter's family enabling them to continue living at Castletown and to keep their horses. The great social event in Ireland was the Dublin Horseshow which lasted a week. Diana asked me to this in 1965, where some 20 of us young were billeted on the top floor of Castletown with only two baths and loos, one of which quickly blocked. However, this scarcely mattered. Each night there was a party with us getting home around 6 a.m. Some of these were wild. There was an unfortunate photo of me in a tabloid drinking from a lady's shoe. This did not amuse my parents when they saw it. Each morning of

1967, Melton Cross Country Race, winner and First Lady, Rosemary Cadell, First Man, PDN.

the show at around 10 a.m we were awoken somewhat bleary eyed by a maid with a pitcher of water which was poured into a bowl for ablutions. Then at Lord Carew's insistence it was off to the show for the day before the next party. While staying at Castletown I met Elizabeth Bacon who was there having been asked by Diana's younger brother Bunny. Some years later it was through Elizabeth that I met Sarah, my wife to be.

Because of winning the Aintree 'Foxhunters' twice I was something of a hero and when hunting with Diana was always mounted on outstanding horses. Irish hunting is very different from English. In the east it is mainly ditches, which require a special technique to cross, consisting of a slow approach then the horses springing like a cat. In the west, it is the famous Irish Banks, while in Galway with the 'Blazers' it is hundreds of small stone walls. It was less formal than most hunting in

England, although a top hat and red coat were the uniform for the 'gentry'.

When I left the army I was on the reserve for a few years but then joined the Northumberland Hussars. This was originally a cavalry regiment but post 1939 had armoured cars. With all my other activities I did not have much time for soldiering although I attended some five TA camps. The Northumberland Hussars drew both officers and men from the North East. I was in the Durham Squadron based at South Shields. Yeomanry soldiering combined some serious military purpose with a great deal of fun and wild mess night parties, during which far too much alcohol was drunk, and severe headaches were too often the norm next morning. The regiment was commanded when I joined by Matthew Ridley, whose father Mat (Viscount) Ridley was honorary Colonel. Matthew looked with tolerance on the wilder antics of some of the younger officers who included his brother Nicholas, subsequently a leading member in Margaret Thatcher's Government. A veil is best drawn over some of the activities we got up to. On one occasion I arrived at camp at Warcop in what was then Cumberland, having just had a heavy fall steeplechasing at Cartmel, one of the most unusual steeplechase courses, where the circuit was less than a mile and each fence was jumped three times in a 3-mile race. I probably had delayed concussion because I was extremely ill that evening, however fortunately recovered quickly. Matthew was succeeded as commanding officer by John (Lord) Barnard, and then by Ralph Carr-Ellison. All of these were subsequently Lord Lieutenants of Northumberland, Durham and Tyne and Wear respectively. In 1966 during the first of many TA reorganizations over the past 35 years the regiment was reduced and I and three other less active officers were retired. I thus never got beyond the undistinguished rank of Lieutenant, having been passed over for Captaincy.

When I was in New York in 1966, I had an introduction to a member of the New York Coaching Club and having written to introduce myself received a wire saying 'come to my party in New Jersey – dress Coaching Club evening dress, pink coat, or black tie for the lower orders'. Having rung my parents, I did get my pink coat and white tie etc over just in time. My host to be, Jack Seabrook, meanwhile told me that I was to be collected by another member of the club, Chauncey Stillman. I spoke to Chauncey whose age I had no idea of, and arranged that he would pick me up in my East 90th street apartment only a few blocks from Harlem, which I was sharing with Johnny (Earl of) Dunmore whom I had met during the course at Harvard, and three others. I waited at the appointed time while a huge Chrysler Imperial drew up, out of which stepped a chauffeur in leggings, and a rather dishevelled little man beside him. From the back emerged a very distinguished man of some 60 years who was obviously my host. I was just about to hand my bags to the dishevelled little man when my host said, 'Do you know Mr Annigoni?' I sat beside my host on the drive to his famous home Weathersfield in upstate New York during which I discovered he had a daughter whom I was introduced to on arrival, a charming but very shy girl. She was to my chagrin not coming to the party, but she did come to my farewell party before I left New York, attended by a billion dollars worth of girls according to one of my flatmates, a Morgan Stanley banker. She possibly made up a substantial portion of this. Later she became a cancer surgeon, and I don't think she was ever comfortable with her father's considerable wealth, inherited from his father who had been an early railroader.

The party itself started with us being driven by George 'Frolic' Weymouth in a 'Unicorn' – a 3-horse vehicle. Frolic is a man who lives life to the full. He is a member of the Du Pont family, but in his own right is one of the finest portrait painters of his generation, and has painted Prince Philip. He lives in Pennsylvania in a 1600s house, one of the oldest inhabited houses in America. He is a legend in his lifetime for his parties, his capacity for mint juleps and for his tremendous sense of fun – a real eccentric. The party host Jack Seabrook has become a lifelong friend. He was President of the Coaching Club of New York when I was President of the British Coaching Club. Now in his eighties he is the most distinguished looking man of his generation and still driving teams of horses.

I don't remember too many details of the actual party, held I believe to celebrate his tenth wedding anniversary, which shows what a good party it was. When the Vaux tragedy occurred and I resigned, I sent a number of friends copies of my resignation statement, and received a charming reply from him, to the effect that he had faced a parallel situation with a company called Seabrook Farms some 40 years earlier, and had received the advice from another friend which he passed on to me – 'Don't cry over spilt milk, don't be bitter, and never look back', advice which he admitted he had not always managed to follow as indeed is my own experience.

My first visit to America which started with an Atlantic crossing on SS *United States* instilled in me a love and admiration of the country and its people. This is something I have never felt for our continental neighbours. For me the Atlantic remains much narrower than the Channel, as I believe it would be for most British people if they were not fed grossly distorted information from much of our media.

I was still riding hard in 1967, but weight was becoming more and more of a problem. A regime of drastic 'fasting' to shed up to two stone each year after Christmas was no longer attractive. Point-to-pointing while fun, particularly if riding a winner, did not have the same thrill as riding at Liverpool where in 1966 I did ride Sea Knight who got round but was not fit enough because he had been lame earlier in the year.

I had dabbled with fast cars, particularly a little Lancia sports car, however when I became a director, the Company provided me with a Jaguar Saloon which was fast but not sporty. I have had a Jaguar ever since. I took up flying in May 1967, a new pursuit, learning at Newcastle Flying Club which was run then by Michael Gill, whose name was still, until recently, used by Gill Airways. The Flying Club had two-seater Cessna 150s, high wing planes with a fixed undercarriage. After obtaining my private pilot's licence in October that year, a friend David Shennan and I invested in a slightly larger four-seater Cessna 172, which I began to use increasingly to fly between Newcastle Airport or Sunderland Airfield, located in 1967 where Nissan now have their car factory, and Edinburgh, for virtually weekly visits to our operations in Scotland. From the North East it was relatively easy to fly low around the coast or if visibility was sufficient, to head for the East of Cheviot, bearing left afterwards to avoid the Otterburn Military Ranges.

There is a saying that there are 'Old Pilots' and 'Bold Pilots', but no 'Old, Bold Pilots'. I did become rather over bold and am lucky now to have become relatively old, although no longer a pilot.

In 1967 and 1968, two friends, Di Davie and Katie Guest took a villa first of all in Portugal and then in Spain, where they invited a number of their friends to join them, on a paying basis. I had met Di through Ronnie Hoare. He was a Cambridge friend living as a tenant of her father in Ayrshire, and working in Glasgow where Vaux's Scottish subsidiary Ushers Brewery of Edinburgh had a substantial depot which I visited frequently. In the late sixties no-one was supposed to take out of the country on holiday more than £50 currency a year and this had to be stamped in one's passport. Di and Katie in order to have enough had to stuff pound notes in their bras to evade customs. Credit cards except in America were rarely used but £50 went a surprisingly long way. After a fun time in Portugal in 1967 travelling conventionally, I was emboldened with my new licence and plane to fly myself down to Malaga. Sue Marr, an old friend, rashly agreed to come with me. I had to get a professional pilot to fly with me into Gatwick but if the weather was clear I would be allowed to fly myself out.

Having over-nighted at Gatwick, it was clear there the next day, but bad weather was forecast across France, meaning that I couldn't legally fly to my planned stop in Toulouse. But after studying weather maps, I reckoned that if I kept to the Atlantic coast, I could fly at a few hundred feet high but under any storms and stop at Bilbao on the Basque Coast. It was a fairly hairy flight under several thunderstorms but we made it with a stop for refuelling. Next day it was clear in Bilbao but there was heavy cloud over the Pyrenees which go up to 6,000 feet south of Bilbao, however the tops of the clouds were forecast to be at 8000 feet, and I thought I could climb up over the sea above the level of the cloud, and once clear of the mountains on the North Coast the forecast was good. We took off and I quickly was in unexpected cloud with a gap appearing to reveal a mountain dead ahead which we were not going to get over. With the stall warning screaming, we circled up and as the altimeter passed 6000 feet I breathed a huge sigh of relief. My companion seemed at that stage remarkably cool. We then 'set sail' for the South of Spain. She however noticed some four hours later that the fuel gauges were reading near empty and we both became increasingly alarmed. I had done my homework on fuel and reckoned that we had an ample safety margin but did throttle back to the most economic possible setting before asking for an expedited approach into Malaga, which fortunately they granted. As we reached the parking stand the engine coughed and died. If a cat has nine lives he would have lost two of them on that flight. So concerned was I that this had happened, that I had the fuel tanks checked on my return, to find that they held several gallons less than they were supposed to. If we had run out of fuel, the plane would have crashed on the southern mountains of Spain. I discovered when landing at Malaga that the Spanish at Bilbao had not forwarded a flight plan so they had no idea we were coming. It could have been days before anyone would have realized we were missing, and then pilot error would have been blamed for allowing the tanks to run dry, if the wreckage was found. It was a lucky escape! I never again flew without allowing a substantial margin for fuel.

Earlier that year I had made a rather more significant flight for my future life. I was riding at the Cambridge University Point-to-Point at Cottenham and flew down to Cambridge. I had taken up an invitation from Elizabeth Bacon whom I had met staying at Castletown to stay at her parents' house in Norfolk. At a late stage she had found that she was unable to go home that weekend but suggested that I went anyway because her sisters would look after

1970, Wedding. Back row, l-r: Nigel (brother), Father, Mother, PDN & Sarah, Lady Bacon, Sir Edmund Bacon, Sir Charles Ponsonby, Lady Ponsonby.

me. There was a small airfield – Seething – close to their house and after my ride I set off in the plane to Seething, but the weather was murky and I couldn't find the field until, just when I was about to give up and head back to Newcastle, I at last spotted it and landed to be met by Lavinia and Sarah Bacon wondering about this strange man their sister had dumped on them.

Sarah came to my 30th birthday dance at Southill but I did not see much of her that year. In the meantime I had been asked to join a skiing party by a girl whom I rather fancied. However I had not realized before I joined the party that she would have a boyfriend there, whom she subsequently married, but more importantly I had failed to take in that she had been in the English women's ski team. She and the rest of the party including her sister with husband were all experts. By the time I arrived, her poor boyfriend in pursuing her down the slopes, had fallen and broken a bone in his bottom and she, when she was not back on the slopes, was ministering cold compresses to this part of his anatomy. However there was a nice French girl who helped me become a little more proficient, to the extent that by the end of the week at Klosters, I did not have to continue to suffer the indignity of coming off the slopes in the lift.

A year or so later I had been asked to join George and Jane Weir with Ronnie Hoare and his then girlfriend in a villa in Italy. I was fortunate to persuade Sarah to come with me in my little plane. Her parents were reluctant to let her come, but on my undertaking to avoid the Alps, relented. Ronnie Hoare joined us and we had some more dramatic moments on that flight, including, while flying under a thunderstorm, finding a mountain ahead that didn't appear on my Italian map. However, subsequently in 1970, Sarah and I were married while Ronnie Hoare the other passenger married her sister Elizabeth two years later.

Before that however, I had decided to upgrade to a twin aircraft. This followed a flight with Sarah from Inverness, where we experienced some alarming 'carburettor icing' above cloud covered Scottish mountains. So it was in a Cessna Skymaster piloted by a friend and with engines at the front and back, that we took off from Norwich after our wedding for our first night in Paris.

Winston Churchill closed his biography of his early days with the words, 'in 1910 I married and lived happily ever after'. In 1970 I did the same.

Chapter 5

The Seventies

MY FATHER HAD RETAINED the lease of 'Quarry Hill' under an agricultural tenancy when he moved after my grandfather died to Southill near Chester-le-Street in 1954. This meant his lease could not be terminated. He had sub-let the house itself, but under a succession of tenants, it had fallen into disrepair partly because of colliery subsidence during the fifties and sixties. I had always preferred Quarry Hill to Southill. Sarah and I were fortunate that the sub tenants were prepared to move in 1970 and thus the house was available to us. However while it was being repaired and done up, our first matrimonial home was a cottage on the farm, and it was there we spent our first few months of married life.

Our daughter Lucy was born in July 1972 just under two years after our wedding, she was to be our only child.

By the time we married, and for the first three and a half years of our married life, there was a nominally Conservative Government under Edward Heath, although many of his policies were well to the left of the current Labour Government. Vaux had seriously stagnated in the years 1965-1969. 1970 the first year of the new government was also the first year of renewed profit growth for Vaux. I was taking increasing responsibility in a company which in 1970 had only 'ad hoc' marketing, no budgets and hardly any contact with city analysts and advisors. My third brother Andrew, having also qualified as a Chartered Accountant, joined Vaux in 1969 and was a great help in persuading an increasingly geriatric board that things could not go on as they were.

We managed to persuade the board of the need for more professional marketing and Peter Heyward was recruited to the company from Guinness. I also managed to introduce new blood, in the shape of Stephen Gibbs, onto the board itself. I had met him through my in-laws. He came from a city PR background and was at the time a supporter and ally in my battle for change. It was just coincidence that he was to marry Sarah's sister in 1972.

Between us we decided that the most effective way to create a climate for change would be to call in outside consultants, as suggestions through such a third party could prove easier to sell. The consultants confirmed the need for proper controls and clear objectives.

There was also the need to communicate these objectives to our major shareholders. I was fortunate that the leading brewery analyst in the City, John Pawle, a partner in brokers Fielding Newson Smith asked to come and see us around that time. John was ahead of his time in developing analysis based on knowledge rather than rumour and gossip. He had made it his business to know everyone in the industry. He was however enormously discreet, so was widely trusted by many who otherwise were sceptical and mistrustful of the city. He confirmed frankly that Vaux had not been well regarded by potential investors for some years.

It was at his instigation, and with his considerable help that the first 'Vaux Open Day' was held in October 1972. Over the next 25 years and particularly in the seventies and early eighties, these set the pace for company/investor communication. They became something of a legend. One leading analyst, John Walters, in his entry in a City reference book listed 'attending the Vaux Open Day' as his main hobby! We set out from the start with the principle that at these events we would present the company 'warts and all', and be very frank in answering questions. In the early years this caused an accusation of divulging inside information. When this began to be an issue, I moved the date of open day to a few days after the Annual General Meeting (AGM). At the AGM I tried to summarize for those attending what the analysts were to be told a few days later. This largely solved such a problem, although it never solved another problem, which was that almost invariably our share price fell next day, as analysts, who were unused to such candour, assumed that problems we revealed were unique to us.

The holding of the first 'open day' concentrated the minds of myself and the senior management to formulate and decide on a coherent strategy for the group, which I could present at the meeting.

Against a background where Vaux in the early 1970s was heavily dependent on beer, and particularly vulnerable to the problems of the North East and Scottish economies, the strategy had three strands. First, this was to develop into associated fields, so that we were not so dependent on UK beer sales. Second, it was to increase our beer market share in our main trading area, and third, to develop in other areas outside our main trading area, but at the same time to remain regional rather than national. We believed that our reputation in our heartland was strengthened by our commitment there. At the time I set the strategy, I told the analysts that the aim not to be national did not preclude us from looking overseas to develop regional companies in other markets, but that we did not see merger or being taken over by a larger company as the long-term way forward.

Earlier in 1972 I had managed to persuade my father to allow me to bring together our diverse range of hotels in England and Scotland under one banner, and a separate 'Swallow' hotels division was set up with a senior manager recruited from Trust Houses. Swallow was originally chosen by my father as a name for a group of country hotels formed just after the Second World War. There were strict rules for these in days of rationing. They had to have their own Red Poll cows to produce milk, and Rhode Island hens for eggs. They also had to have Corgi dogs and Siamese cats, this was his eccentricity! He chose the name because swallows return to the same nest year after year, provided they are happy! By the sixties we had begun to develop and build slightly more urban concepts, the first being the Golden Circle at Bathgate, Scotland. The first hotel actually named 'Swallow' opened in Newcastle in 1969. It was my initial experience of a major construction project and the problems of controlling contractors, and cost, lessons which were not lost, although we had one other major disaster in this area, many years later in Bristol. This happened just at the time in 1990 the hotel industry went into the third and most serious recession of my years with the company.

Another change I initiated in 1972 was the idea of a long-range plan trying to set specific objectives over the next five years. The plan was meant to come in from the start of the Companies 1973/74 year on 1 May and while this timetable slipped a little we were able to introduce for the first time a detailed and integrated budget covering both capital and revenue.

The other major area which required new thinking was 'human resources'. I was much influenced by the teachings of the Industrial Society, under an inspirational leader, John Garnett. He developed such ideas as briefing groups, works councils, and the need to identify more closely the interests of employees and shareholders. The seventies were an era of high inflation and industrial turmoil. We largely avoided the latter and indeed gained considerable competitive advantage from the problems others faced in this area.

I had officially become joint managing director with my father, who remained Chairman, in 1971. I am grateful that he allowed me an increasing degree of control, something that did not come easily to him, but fortunately he was much diverted at that time, participating in the new sport of 'Combined Driving' of horse drawn carriages. While these were Vaux horses, he believed, and I was not to gainsay him, that the publicity value of their success more than offset the cost to the company. The Vaux horses in Sunderland were something of an icon. They represented continuity and tradition. I had a feeling that, like the ravens in the tower, should they ever go, that would be the end. They went in April 1999 four months before the brewery was destroyed. Anyhow his driving activities, where in 1972 he had been part of the winning British Team in the first World Driving Championships, held in Hungary, left me to get on with running the 'shop', including such important matters as writing the chairman's statement for the accounts. It was only in 1972 that this was first published with the accounts rather than being given at the AGM.

Having set the strategy the company moved forward. It changed its name in 1973 from the cumbersome 'Vaux and Associated Breweries Ltd', to the snappier 'Vaux Breweries Ltd'. It was the second largest company with its ultimate headquarters in the North East, having late in 1972 acquired S.H. Ward & Company of Sheffield.

I believed at the time that it was right to have senior executives in the company on the board and managed to persuade my father to appoint three. The offer of an appointment to Michael Wright was an implied condition of our acquisition of Wards, but if he was to join the board it was only right that the other two senior managers in the group, Hamish Inglis running our Scottish subsidiary at the time, known as 'Ushers', and my brother Andrew who was mainly responsible for all Sunderland production matters, should also join. It is interesting however how fashions change. At the time it did not cross my mind or that of any of my colleagues that we also needed a Finance Director on the board.

The acquisition of Wards was a major development for the group. In early 1972, as I was forming our strategy, Peter Heyward and I arranged a tour visiting three smaller brewery companies on the periphery of our area. These were T.B. Darley and Sons of Thorne near Doncaster, run by Thomas Darley, who was by then into his seventies and had no apparent successor, and S.H. Ward and Co of Sheffield, where the Wright family who ran it had 51% of the shares between 11 members and the Ward family had 49%. The third brewery we visited was Holts Brewery in Manchester, but there the family was clearly not going to seek an 'out' at any stage, and it is good that 30 years later, the Kershaws, who have run it father and sons for several generations, were able to take the company private. When we came back from our tour, Peter and I thought that eventually we might be able to buy Darleys but were doubtful about Wards.

Some months later Michael Wright, son of the Wards chairman, came to tell me that the Ward family had sold their 49% stake to

Trumans, by then owned by the feared takeover king Maxwell Joseph. His minions had then made a presumptuous demand to the Wrights to sell out. Michael had a problem in that the Wrights' stake was divided among some eleven family members some of whom were not close to the rest, but if any had broken ranks then Joseph would have obtained 50% and control. Wards would almost certainly then have then been shut, and those Wrights working in the company out of a job.

Earlier that year I had appointed as advisors a young Scottish Merchant Bank, Noble Grossart whose co-founder Angus Grossart, I had met a few times and through whom we had just bought Lowlands of Scotland Hotels, a small Scottish hotel and pub company with some 13 outlets. I consulted him, and he assigned Peter Stevenson, brother of Dennis Stevenson (now Lord Stevenson of Coddenham) to help us. There followed some delicate and secret negotiations to buy out all eleven Wrights. It was essential that the other side did not get wind of what was going on, or they might have upped the price beyond our resources. Fortunately those Wrights actually in the business were more interested in the preservation of the company than maximizing the price, and they were able to hold their cousins to sign an irrevocable agreement to sell us the 51%.

Maxwell Joseph was always a realist. Acknowledging he would not get control, he sought his pound of flesh. We had to buy out his 49% for rather more than what we had paid the Wrights, considerably to the chagrin of Wright family members not actually in the Company. Joseph had threatened otherwise just to sit on the 49%, which was the last thing we needed in Vaux!

Our first year of married life was a busy one on the social front as well as at work. The Coaching Club held its Centenary Meet at Hampton Court on June 22nd 1971. At that stage Vaux had eight Gelderlander carriage horses so I was able to drive for the first time at an official meet alongside my father. The Coaching Club have a rule, that when driving a coach at an official meet and the member's wife is on board, she must sit beside the member so that no lady or 'whip' (as the driver is called) is tempted with adulterous thoughts! We had as our guests that evening two couples, Alan and Camilla Abbot Anderson, a well known actress who starred in a TV series called 'The Power Game' where she played the role of PA to the boss. The other couple were Alan and Tara Elliot.

Alan and Tara have been with us since on many coaching occasions. Alan, known to all his friends as 'Ikey' – he even signs himself such, is actually a staunch Roman Catholic. He is a larger than life character of great generosity but very competitive and tact has never been his strongest point. He has managed the unusual feat of making serious money as an entrepreneur while enjoying a hectic and unceasing social life. Imposing of presence, some find him intimidating and he is not without enemies. But to their friends, of whom there are many, he and Tara are very special people and we have enjoyed great fun over the years, either on holiday together or as their guests in the sun or on the shooting field.

It was shortly after the Coaching Club meet that we joined his party in a house he had rented from his brother at Soto Grande in Southern Spain. Now as I was flying a Skymaster with two engines, the flight out was rather less traumatic than my 1968 flight to Malaga. The only incident on the way out was being held up nearly an hour circling near Malaga while the then American Vice President, Spiro Agnew, was leaving on Air Force 2. Sarah and I only had basically beach clothes and nothing smart, so it was more than a little off putting to find how smart the rest of the party was. One French lady remarked to Sarah, 'It is really so silly that we wear in Soto Grande the same as we wear in Paris!'.

On the way back we stopped in Gerona to go walking in the Pyrenees. From there we had just taken off on what should have been our return trip, when Sarah noticed that the oil gauge on one of the engines was reading zero. In my panic I nearly feathered the wrong engine, however, that sorted out we landed back at Gerona and eventually found a Cessna Agent who could effect the necessary repairs, albeit it would take months. We managed to find two seats on a charter back to Manchester, but it was nearly three months before I eventually saw the plane back and I again had it available for my, at the time, weekly trip to our Scottish operation.

1973 and 1974 were traumatic years for Britain. The miners' strike brought down the Heath Government. The stock market slid and then crashed. Inflation soared. Interest rates were 15% although in real terms negative. However on the personal side, in spite of all the gloom and doom, with statements from the Government that they intended to squeeze the rich until the pips squeaked, things went on much as before. In February 1973 Sarah and I had paid our first of many visits to Thailand. We also went that summer to Calabria for a recuperative holiday after Sarah had undergone a serious operation. We went to Thailand with George and Jane Weir and Graham Gillies. George, a member of the Weir engineering family, had probably the brightest brain of any of my contemporaries. After Cambridge he had obtained a Doctorate from Massachusetts Institute of Technology. He sadly died of cancer in 2001 but had not had a very happy time either personally or financially in recent years. In earlier times he was excellent company, and had an enormous circle of friends. His marriage was to fall apart, although he and Jane came together again after her second husband died.

We managed each year to fit in a few days deer stalking mainly with Jimmy Ferard, a Harrow and army friend in the insurance business, who took Corrour, a 100,000-acre deer forest north of Rannoch which until the late sixties was only accessible by train. The Fort William sleeper from London stopped some three miles down the loch from the lodge. The original lodge had been burnt down pre-war, and replaced post-war by a wooden construction. This in contrast to most Scottish lodges was warm and comfortable.

On some occasions I took Corrour personally and had my own guests including Jimmy Ferard and Paul Goudime, a boisterous extrovert friend, who when we were together, was known as 'little Paul'. One year I had asked Menzies (Ming) Campbell, another friend who in his early days as a sprinter was one of the fastest white men on earth. Now he is a leading Liberal politician. On this occasion, I had sent Paul who had arrived overnight on the sleeper straight out on the hill, accompanied by Ming. Paul led a typical City of London existence, hardly designed to make him fit. However at the end of the day, he almost had to carry the great athlete Ming home!

In the Spring of 1974 we were on holiday in North Cyprus, just after the change of Government. A much feared budget was due to be presented while we were away. To protect our much reduced family wealth, I had to arrange to break up my father's trust, which otherwise could have been seriously damaged by tax changes. It was somewhat complicated to do this from North Cyprus even though at that time the island was still unified. However this was achieved, and the ravages at least of the Government, if not the stock market, where Vaux shares actually fell below par to the equivalent of 9p, were mitigated.

I commented in our long-range plan of that year, that 'not in my lifetime had there been so much difficulty and uncertainty'. However in spite of a slump in our hotel division and the Sunderland Breweries main boiler blowing up in October 1974, we actually increased profits for that year.

The uncertain economy did not stop us from seeking our first venture overseas, which was in Belgium, where after looking at a number of breweries we bought 'Liefmans' a small brewery based in Oudenaarde. Peter Stevenson of Noble Grossart and I had earlier examined a number of opportunities. At one such we were entertained by the proprietor, who hoping to make a sale, produced for lunch a bottle of Latour 1927 claret. We duly expressed our appreciation of his generosity, at which his son was dispatched to his cellar and appeared with a bottle of the 1908 vintage, which was delicious. I think the proprietor was very disappointed not to make the sale!

Fortunately the stock market which hit its low the day Burmah Oil went bust, bounced back quickly, doubling in a matter of weeks. The Conservative government under Heath, which had been overthrown, was actually one of the most socialist this country had ever experienced, with its introduction of draconian prices and incomes policies and the maintenance of high personal levels of taxation inherited from the 1960s. It was however possible to do business in spite of problems caused by the incoming Labour Government kow-towing to the unions and fuelling ever higher inflation. Price controls meant that everyone concentrated on achieving the maximum allowed increase. Ironically with competition subdued thereby, prices rose faster than they might otherwise have done.

1975 was the year of the referendum to confirm our acceptance of the Common Market and the European Economic Community. Many of us who voted enthusiastically for these concepts would have taken a very different view if it had been a European Union with a single currency. Few of us understood what we were really letting themselves in for! At the time I wrote an article for the *Sunderland Echo* urging a yes vote because I believed strongly in free trade.

I had an unpleasant experience that year with a high profile brush with the law. Durham City had had long-term plans to re-align Elvet Bridge, including the demolition of some 18th century buildings adjacent to the Three Tuns hotel which belonged to Vaux. We had thus done nothing to maintain these buildings. I received a report that the buildings were in imminent danger of collapse onto Elvet with potentially catastrophic consequences. The local authority were consulted but the bureaucracy couldn't appreciate the urgency of the situation, so I ordered their demolition.

At this the conservation lobby, which was powerful in Durham and had indeed done a good job in the past, rose up in arms. They persuaded the local authority to take criminal proceedings not just against the company, but against me personally, and against John Snowden whose firm did the demolition.

QCs were engaged on both sides, on my side I had Gilbert Gray QC. Originally the prosecuting counsel was to be Peter Taylor QC who became subsequently Lord Chief Justice, but he backed out and his replacement was Humphrey Potts QC, recently much in the news as the judge in the Lord Archer trial. The case came before the magistrates. Somewhat embarrassed they asked me if I wanted to sit with my counsel, but I declined, insisting on sitting in the Dock.

It was a most unpleasant experience to be cross-examined by someone trying to impugn my motives and blacken everything I said. At the end of a three-day hearing, the magistrates adjourned their verdict. My QC remarked 'if they find you guilty, it is a fix', a month later I was found guilty. Although personally given an absolute discharge, the company was fined £10,000, a not insignificant sum in those days and equivalent to over £60,000 today.

On appeal Humphrey Potts and I both lost our temper, and were each rebuked by the judge, who in his summing up said that Mr Nicholson acted properly in the situation, but was still guilty as the offence was absolute! Many years later Humphrey Potts told me the real driver of the prosecution was his junior, a certain Leo Blair!

Throughout the early seventies we were trading well in England, but with problems in Scotland where we were squeezed between Scottish Brewers and the Bass subsidiary, Tennants. Our introduction of Norseman lager in 1973, initially appeared successful but proved to be a flash in the pan. Our problems were that the breweries we had acquired in the fifties Steele Coulson and Co, and Thomas Usher had poor reputations and we probably did not do enough to improve product quality and reliability. We had a good reputation for our pubs, but a lousy one for beer. We had one good brand 'Lorimers', brewed in a separate brewery acquired by my grandfather personally in 1919 when the Vaux family refused to buy it. He had sold this to the company in 1947, but almost all its production came to England. However 1975 was a reasonable year by the then standards, with a 13% increase in profit but a 19% increase in the cost of living. In real terms we went backwards, but we were outperforming most of our competitors.

Over that year my father developed the distressing symptoms of what we knew later was Alzheimer's. He had over 40 years earlier suffered a near fatal head injury losing the main blood vessel in his head. While he had appeared to recover fully from this, it was probably the cause of what was to happen to him. His behaviour became increasingly eccentric and eventually, supported by my brother Andrew, I had to tell him he must go. It was a difficult personal time and initially he thought I was betraying him, however eventually he accepted the situation and made a dignified and moving statement at the 1976 AGM. He remained on the board for a time but deteriorated fairly quickly and within two years his mind had more or less ceased. I was very lucky to have a father who, while not an easy man and very strong minded, was always a support when needed and once convinced of a situation then backed me fully. I therefore became Chairman at the AGM in August 1976, a position I held until my resignation in March 1999. For most of that time, up until August 1998 I was also Chief Executive.

Over the previous five years Vaux had developed successfully in circumstances very different from today. At our 'Open Day' that year I told the assembled City representatives in Sunderland,

> I am sure you all realize, that we in industry have to face many directions at once to deal with different interest groups. I think this is no bad thing. I believe with the greatest respect to you gentlemen that the interests of those working for us can sometimes be as, or more, important than maximizing profit. A company based in this town (Sunderland), with its 14% male unemployment is very conscious of the needs of the area. Unfortunately most of the companies in this area are mere subsidiaries of concerns based elsewhere, and this could be one of the reasons why the North East, and much of Scotland has suffered. I would fight fiercely to preserve this independence, if this was threatened by a predator from outside.

Against a background of frequent speculations about the future of Vaux, few would have prophesied we would actually last another twenty three years and be successful over that period.

My initial time taking over the reins at Vaux had matured me, but also given me a strong feeling that I should try and do what I could for the region at large. First and foremost I believed that maintenance of Vaux in Sunderland was the biggest contribution I could make, but having established the basic aims of the Group, and given it a platform to move forward, I was beginning to become involved in the affairs of the region.

I had been furious with the CBI when its then Director General, in 1974, at a crucial stage in the election run up that year, made a statement which was extremely unhelpful to the embattled Conservative Government. This had possibly tipped the balance to Labour in an election where the Conservatives actually polled more votes than Labour in spite of losing.

Rather than resign from the CBI I had joined their Northern Regional Council in 1976, and just over a year later was asked to be Chairman of that Council. This was my introduction to the wider aspects of the region. While it did take up a considerable amount of time, I believed that by devoting energy to activities connected with the prosperity of the North East, I could make what I hoped might be a valuable contribution to some of the problems. A more prosperous North East would mean a more prosperous Vaux.

A more prosperous Vaux was achieved over the next few years. We benefited strongly from our good labour relations, at a time when competitors had frequent strikes. Our good labour relations were not however a matter of chance. I probably devoted at least half my time to such initiatives as profit share schemes, developing brewery and retail councils, and introducing briefing groups. It was an era of extreme inflation, making labour relations exceptionally difficult, particularly as the then Government had introduced laws giving ever more power to Unions. I myself actually got on well with the local union organizers. We had recognized the Transport and General in 1978 when a majority of those involved voted for it, but it was done without confrontation and they understood our belief that direct communications with employees was crucial.

Another of Vaux's strengths was in the working men's club sector of the beer trade, but in the seventies competition became fiercer and some competitors resorted to what amounted to bribery of club stewards and committees. I was so concerned at this that I instigated a meeting of the chairmen of the major brewers at the Portman Square offices of the Brewers Society. Not surprisingly the chairmen denied all knowledge of such happenings, which were probably going on at levels well beneath their normal gaze, but my implied threats to take the matter further unless the practice stopped, largely had the desired affect!

Contrary to what many believed, the brewing industry was highly competitive. However because of the problems of alcohol and licensing legislation, it was always necessary to have a powerful trade association to fight the common cause on such issues as beer duty, licensing laws and ensuring rationality on alcohol matters. As a result we as brewers all knew each other and in many cases were friends, but this did not stop fierce competition, where in Scotland we were to be defeated.

There we had decided on a change of name to 'Lorimers' in 1976, hoping that this might correct the image, but when this did not work, I decided to try a change of management, and Hamish Inglis managing director of Lorimers left us. Hamish had probably, with hindsight, been asked to achieve the near impossible. He was replaced by David Hart and it became increasingly obvious that if we could find a buyer for our Scottish Brewing and Pubs operation, then we should exit.

Our year ended September 1978 was very successful with over 30% increase in pound note profits although against the background of 15% inflation.

During this time there were a number of management changes. My brother Andrew decided he wanted to fulfil his long-held ambition to be a farmer, and became non-executive. Later he left the board when he spent some years in Australia, before coming back to educate his children over here and setting up in business as a head-hunter. We recruited Richard Pettit from British Leyland. Richard was an original thinker and particularly good at industrial relations. He made a significant contribution to the company during his time with us by challenging all aspects of our thinking, always with good humour. It was sad that for personal reasons he had to leave us in 1984.

By the time I came to write the 1979 report one of the most fundamental changes in British history had got underway. The Labour Government reaped a whirlwind from what it had sown by its appeasement of unions in the 1978 winter of discontent. In May of 1979 Margaret Thatcher was elected Prime Minister. Top rate taxes were slashed from 98%, for so called unearned income (83% for earned income), first to 60% and later to 40%. Managers began to get back the power to manage and life through the eighties was very different from the seventies. Controls on prices, incomes and dividends – such a feature of the seventies – were abolished, but so also were excuses for failure.

My spell from September 1977 to 1979 as Chairman of the Northern Region of CBI gave me a considerable insight into what was going on. For a time I was Chairman of the Regional Chairmen's Group of CBI, a post which rotated every six months and as such I was a member of the inner sanctum of the CBI – the President's Council. In the latter stages of the Callaghan Government, I was part of a CBI delegation to Downing Street on 17th July, 1978, memorable for a statement from the Prime Minister that over his dead body would inflation again exceed 10%. This it promptly did! It was also memorable for me, seeing the rubicund face of the Chancellor, Denis Healey. Our delegation all thought he would not long survive, he looked so ill. How wrong we were – he is still with us some 25 years later!

The CBI was itself infected with the corporate vices of the age. I had a major row with John Methven the great Director General over the issue of whether the CBI should promote greater employer solidarity against trade unions. My argument was that this just would not work in a free enterprise society. The answer was not to promote solidarity as a corrective to an imbalance of power, but rather to concentrate all efforts on bringing unions back within the law. Few believed at the time, this would be possible. How wrong they were to prove.

As I began to have a rather higher North East profile outside the company, Sarah and I also managed to have fun with our growing daughter who in 1977 started in a state primary school in Durham. Some of her classmates there have remained friends to this day. We did not have a full-time child minder, but my old nanny Jean Chrisp, and later another retired nanny, were available to look after her when we were away, which meant we could enjoy visits to interesting countries and with friends. Ming and Elspeth Campbell came with us to Italy in 1974 while in 1975 we went again to Thailand with George and Jane Weir and Graham Gillies. In 1976 we went with Angus Grossart to Marrakech. Angus was still a bachelor and much in demand both commercially and romantically as his bank was going from strength to strength.

In 1977 Jubilee year, Sir John Miller, the Crown Equerry and also President of the Coaching Club asked if we could lend horses for the Lord Mayor's procession to the St Paul's Silver Jubilee service. My father and I each drove a pair. It was almost the last time he drove before his disease became too far advanced. We drove from the Palace Mews to the Mansion House where we picked up our charges. We were not actually driving the Lord Mayor himself but some of his Aldermen. I feel privileged to have taken part not just in the Coronation, but in the Silver Jubilee, while for the Golden Jubilee we were in St Paul's itself, sitting some ten rows back from the Queen. I do not think there are many others outside the Royal family who can claim to have had a part in all three events.

After father's retirement, I tried to continue his tradition of showing the Vaux horses, particularly at the Royal Show. In the seventies I did not have much success and I can remember the then Vaux Head Coachman, Jimmy Peach, telling me rather pointedly when we had come fourth, that he had never had a rosette as low as fourth in his life. Fortunately I did rather better in the eighties and nineties.

I was still flying myself through the seventies. I had passed my instrument rating in 1974. By that time the aircraft I was flying was a Piper Twin Comanche which was a fast but quite tricky twin-engined plane. I replaced this in 1977 with a rather more

1977, Preparing to Drive in the Lord Mayor's Procession at Silver Jubilee.

substantial and forgiving twin – a Beech Baron. As the plane belonged to Vaux, we didn't use it for overseas holidays but I sometimes flew it to Belgium and frequently to Scotland or London landing at Elstree or Leavesden aerodromes.

In 1978 I celebrated my fortieth birthday with a summer dinner and dance at Quarry Hill held in a marquee with a steel band. It was easy to organize, as Vaux had an excellent outside catering department, run by Alan Lishman of Swallow Hotels, which for years catered for some prestigious events such as the Governor's tent at the Royal Show. It was not very profitable but good advertising.

Over the previous years Sarah and I had developed a wide circle of friends, many of whom were among our one hundred and fifty guests on this occasion, and twenty five years later are still part of our lives, particularly through shooting.

In 1976 it was becoming clear that deer stalking at Corrour was not going to be possible much longer. We looked around for alternatives and Sarah spotted in the back of the *Times* an advertisement of a West Highland cottage for sale with the possibility of rented deer stalking. At the end of that glorious summer we flew up to Aberdeen where I had business, then hired a car and drove across to Diabaig on the West Coast, where both Sarah and I fell in love with the beauty of the place. There was one problem however to overcome, before we could conclude a deal, in that the Laird of the property, Brigadier MacKenzie of Gairloch – a formidable highland chieftain – had to approve us as tenants. With some trepidation Sarah and I went to be interviewed by him. However it all went well. The Brigadier was mainly interested in which of his friends knew our respective fathers. We passed muster and jointly with Sarah's brother Nicholas Bacon, we bought the property and took a 15-year lease on the 17,000 acres of stalking attached.

Our first year in occupation was 1977, I lent the property for August to my parents and younger brothers, arranging to go up ourselves at the end of that month when we had invited one of Sarah's sisters and her husband, the Gibbses, to join us. At the last moment they had cried off, but on the evening before we were going, we had been invited to a dinner by Anthony and Daphne Scott Harden, who owned grouse moors near Blanchland and were entertaining a Swiss American party of guns, to whom they had let their shooting.

At dinner that night I asked my neighbour, a Californian, Barbara Carlsberg, what they were planning to do after shooting. She told me they were going to hire a car and drive around Scotland. I suggested to her that she and her husband Dick should come and join us. She accepted the invitation and that chance conversation was to have profound and very pleasurable consequences for our lives over the next nearly 20 years.

They came. It turned out that Dick was a mighty hunter who had shot big game all over the world. However when I took him stalking, lending him my rifle, a David Lloyd .243, he only grazed the stag he fired at. He was so upset that that night, after we had consumed most of the contents of a bottle of whisky, he told me he did not think much of 'that little pop gun of yours', and he was going to send me a proper rifle.

Some weeks later he faxed me to say that one of his representatives was coming to the UK and was bringing me a rifle. Even in 1977, firearm laws were strict, and the problem was how to bring this in. It happened that his colleague was arriving from Los Angeles at Gatwick while I was attending the first CBI conference at Brighton. As Chairman of CBI Northern Region, I packed a little punch and managed to organize through the police in the North East and the Gatwick customs that I could meet this representative airside. However somehow we missed each other. He was part of a large party, and all their bags including my rifle were whisked through customs onto their bus for central London.

At that the Gatwick police became seriously alarmed, and as a result the poor man was woken in the middle of the night and nearly arrested while the rifle was confiscated. However eventually it was sorted out, and I became the proud possessor of a Weatherby .270, which John Orr, then Chief Constable of the Lothians and a rifle expert told me, was the absolute 'Rolls Royce' of rifles. I have used it ever since. It is a very lethal weapon, the only problem being that it has an upward kick. It is easy to catch one's eyebrow on the telescope when firing a shot. Apparently the resultant scar is known in American hunting circles as a 'Weatherby eyebrow'. I do now possess this!

The Carlsbergs became enormous friends and through introducing me to an organization called the 'Young Presidents' have had a profound effect on my subsequent business and social life, as is related in subsequent chapters. They came back many times to Diabaig and themselves rented estates in Scotland.

From 1978 through the eighties we usually spent a few weeks in August and sometimes a few days in October at Diabaig.

We had a number of friends who joined us with their growing families, particularly David and Claire Griffith and their daughters. David, a member of the Greenall brewing family, represented their company known then as 'Greenall Whitley' at the 'Brewers Society'. For some 20 years he and I sat next to each other each month on the executive committee of the Society.

His family home is a property in North Wales on which he has a spectacular high pheasant shoot. After lunch he has a sweepstake, not as to the number that will actually be shot, but as to the number of cartridges which will be fired for each bird. This ranges between four where the team are very good shots up to nine with a team of lesser shots like myself.

It was shooting with him that I committed the most terrible faux pas. After lunching rather too well I was placed in a stand just by the house. The birds poured over me and I thought I was shooting rather well. Then one bird landed with a sickening thud. I had shot one of their peahens! I was covered with confusion. Eventually I found a replacement, having scoured the country for dealers in peacocks. I gather the peahen actually tasted delicious and, surprisingly, I have been asked back again!

The seventies were personally and professionally successful and fun years. This was in spite of the Labour Government with its extreme personal taxes, and such horrors as exchange controls limiting the amount of currency that could be taken from the country. While credit cards made these increasingly hard to enforce, my 1979 passport solemnly records with two separate bank authorized stamps that in October 1979, I took £40 out. What bureaucracy!

Chapter 6

On My Travels

On Dick Carlsberg's third return visit he commented to me that he was surprised I was not a member of the 'Young Presidents Organization'. I had to confess that I had never heard of it. He explained that it was an organization set up in the fifties in the United States for chief executives (in American parlance 'presidents') of companies who had reached such a position before the age of 40. The idea was that through idea exchange and education, members would become better 'presidents'. The organization had expanded internationally and there was a London branch called a 'Chapter'.

The main means of achieving the aims of the organization apart from Chapter meetings were international gatherings called 'Universities'. These were week long events where leaders in business, politics and many other fields gave classes. YPO was 'spouse orientated'. It was expected that members not all of whom were male would bring their wife/husband or partner (of the opposite sex – they were not that broadminded!). I made some enquiries and joined to see what it was like. Our first University was in Singapore in 1981. It was a fascinating experience both from a business point of view and socially with its multinational mix of youngish 'Presidents'. Each day was split into 4 or 5 sessions and for each session there was a choice of classes covering subjects as broad as the latest Harvard Business School thinking, to how to improve sex life! Dick introduced us there to Bill and Nadine Tilley. Bill is in the restaurant business and was over the next few years very helpful both in exposing our retail operatives to American thinking and as a shrewd sounding board. We enjoyed ourselves so much in Singapore that we were to attend another nine 'Universities' before I reached the compulsory retirement age of 50.

At our second University we met a genuine business eccentric – the Welshman Christopher Bailey, whose great claim to fame was, that he had found a means of frustrating the Labour Government when they tried to nationalize his ship repair business. Christopher had a beard like Moses, and once managed to infiltrate the security guards protecting President Bush senior in Bermuda by pretending to be an Orthodox Archbishop. The President is reputed to have kissed his ring before the hoax was exposed, which amused him so much that Christopher was invited to the White House. In the eighties and early nineties, Christopher had a yacht charter company of 1920 style 'gin palaces'. We were lucky enough to enjoy some hilarious cruises with him. The boats carried 12 plus passengers with an equal sized crew and were the height of luxury.

It was a great shock to his many friends around the world when he died in September 2002, following a hip replacement operation. Christopher was a character with a capital 'C'. In many respects he was totally unconventional but he could look splendidly Victorian dressed in top hat and tails with his bushy beard when riding on my coach to Ascot. Many, including Margaret Thatcher, appreciated his original thinking. His only direct venture into politics was when he stood as a liberal candidate for a Welsh constituency in one of the 1970s general elections. He did not endear himself to that party when, in the middle of the campaign, he invited his constituents to vote for the Conservative candidate rather than himself.

Our highlight in YPO was being on the committee and running the so called 'cultural' side of a University in Bangkok. The committee consisted apart from myself, of an equal number of Thais and Americans. It was a real clash of cultures, the Americans wanting everything sorted yesterday and the Thais, while perfectly efficient, being very laid back. Sarah and I needed some diplomatic skills finding common ground. At the end of the University the Thai joint Chairman, a leading Far East banker, Sunthorn Arunanondchai announced he was proposing to send his two daughters to school in England and when we gingerly enquired where, he told us he thought they should come to our daughter's school, then the Mount at York. Initially the two girls found the going tough but soon thrived as they were very bright. Ironically some 16 years later the eldest only went back to Thailand a few months ago, having been to university here and then worked in the City in corporate finance. The younger, who now speaks English without even the trace of an overseas accent, recently followed her sister home. Like so many of their English contemporaries, neither has married, much to their parents' chagrin.

Before the Bangkok University Sarah and I took a party of 50 attendees on a pre University tour to Northern Thailand. I had some six months earlier been on a recce tour of the Hill Tribes area to which we were planning to take the party. On asking about drugs, I was given a wedge of pure opium. I had put this in my hand luggage and forgotten about it until half way from Bangkok to Melbourne where I was headed on business. I remembered and knowing the Australian attitude to drugs, flushed the offending object down the aircraft loo. Some days later there was a story in the local paper about the discovery of drugs in a Qantas toilet. I hope they were not mine!

While on a business visit to the States Dick Carlsberg invited me to join his '3-Shot Honker Hunt' to shoot Canada geese in Northern California. It was a great party. Some 50 males assembled in Reno where I remember my hotel room ceiling was a mirror. Presumably this was for some form of titillating coupling, to celebrate or compensate for success or otherwise on the gaming tables, which were also part of the hotel complex.

After a party that night, we all embarked on a bus for a 'Clay Honker Hunt' – a clay pigeon competition in the Nevada Hills. Dick had lent me a 'side by side' gun, as he thought this was more what I was used to, as indeed it was, compared to the pump action or automatic single barrel shot gun most of the rest were using. In spite of this I was not in the prize money for the Clay Honker Hunt. However we then travelled to Dick's Ranch in Northern California where we were to be billeted in dormitory accommodation for the actual Hunt itself. The party included a number of famous American names such as Chuck Jaeger the first pilot to break the sound barrier and particularly General James B Doolittle. General James B, by then in his late seventies, was legendary in America as the first man to bomb Tokyo. After a convivial party the night before, we were awoken around 4.00 a.m. and despatched in groups of three or four guns to various locations around Northern California for the 'Hunt'. Each 'Hunter' was allowed three shots and obviously a 'perfect' was three 'Honkers'. With the exception of General James B, hardly any achieved this. I did manage to bring down one goose, and at the evening prize giving, where awards were given for the biggest 'Honker', the fattest 'Honker' etc, I won the consolation award of a rubber model of a goose for the 'Hunter' who had travelled the furthest for the event! Dick apparently had this party every year for the 20 years before his death. I was never able to fit in another visit to the States at the right time.

I had some testing moments during the latter half of the eighties but Sarah and I also had our share of fun. We attended YPO 'Universities' in a number of exotic locations such as Delhi, Acapulco and Buenos Aires. At one University held in Vale Colorado, Sarah and I finally began to have confidence on skis. We had earlier taken our daughter to Flaine in France during the 1986 Easter holiday, but in the week we were there, we did not make a lot of progress.

After I was fifty in 1988, I could no longer take part in the main Young Presidents Organization, although I was elected to the Chief Executives Organization (CEO) which describes itself as the 'graduate' organization for YPO. I was however able to remain a 49er member of the International Chapter of YPO. To qualify for this Chapter potential members had to have businesses in more than one country. At the time of my election (1985) to this Chapter, I qualified because Vaux had businesses in America, Australia and Belgium.

Those who are active in this Chapter can be invited to stay on after 50. The International Chapter has events which take members to places and to meet people whom they would not be likely to meet otherwise. We organized an event in Scotland where they met Malcolm Rifkind, then Secretary of State, and Willie Whitelaw. We also helped organize an event in London where among others they met the Princess Royal and Margaret Thatcher. I was able to organize for all of them to be taken to Royal Ascot by coach and four, dressed appropriately for the Royal Enclosure. The Americans particularly were overawed.

We attended Jack Seabrook's 70th birthday dance in New Jersey in 1987. As well as being a great 'Whip', Jack had been a highly successful businessman and head of a major corporation. Fellow guests were from the highest echelons of the American East Coast establishment as well as from the horse driving world on both sides of the Atlantic. The 'horsey guests' were invited the next day to join a carriage drive organized by 'Frolic' Weymouth around his Pennsylvanian Estate. We were liberally entertained with his famous 'Mint Juleps' before we set off. Sarah and I were passengers in the lead carriage with Frolic himself as the Whip. He had laid on a variety of distractions and entertainments for those taking part. We came round one corner to find a stark naked girl standing full frontal and gently hoeing the soil. It was not a warm day and we could see the goose-pimples as well as everything else! One of the Whips, possibly overexcited by all this, lost control of his horses while crossing a river. They bolted and he and his unfortunate passengers were tipped into the river when the carriage overturned. By a miracle no one was hurt but the carriage was smashed. I was glad that Sarah and I as passengers were driven by an experienced Whip.

The year 1990 saw our daughter Lucy reach the age of 18 and finish her schooling. She had attended two primary schools in Durham before going off at the age of 11 to The Mount, a Girls' Quaker Boarding School in York. The Mount has children from all over the world. One of Lucy's great friends was 'Nee', daughter of a Nigerian businessman who unfortunately fell out with the then regime, whereupon 'Nee' disappeared from the school. She did resurface many years later when she turned up in London on a Guinness Study Scholarship.

The Quaker influence gives the Mount School pupils a high sense of social responsibility and it may have been this which prompted our daughter to apply to an organization called 'Gap Activity Projects' for one of their positions teaching deprived children in Mexico during her Gap Year. There she became fluent in Spanish. This has proved valuable to her in her career, where she now is Manager of the Latin American section of Cox and Kings, the travel agents. She graduated from the University of Manchester Institute of Science and Technology (UMIST) with a degree in Business Studies in 1993.

Sarah and I have visited some 50 countries for business or pleasure, over the past 30 years. We have had some memorable holidays, particularly in Australia where Lizard Island on the Barrier Reef is a near paradise. One holiday, which was especially memorable for us, was to Chile and the Galapagos in 1990. In company with great friends Alan and Tara Elliot, we met up with Sebastian Santa Cruz, son of a former Chilean Ambassador to Britain, to stay at the Hotel Antunalal on Lake Villarica, where the Queen and Prince Philip had stayed in the sixties, some hundreds of miles south of Santiago. The prime purpose of this part of the trip was fishing, and for two days we trolled for trout with minimal success. However behind Villarica towered 'El Vulcan Villarica', an active volcano which had last erupted some 10 years before, but from which, wisps of steam could be seen from the lake. I decided to climb 'El Vulcan', and through Sebastian, arranged to join a climbing party with a guide, in the local town of Pucon. There I met the rest of the party, consisting of two Spanish men aged about 25, and two German girls who were rather younger. They all spoke fluent Spanish. The guide did not speak English, but from the back of his truck, he produced haversacks, ice axes, crampons and gloves. He had climbing boots available but none of his fitted me, so I decided to climb in my trainers. El Vulcan Villarica is also a ski resort, and we had expected to go part of the way on the ski lift. However this was out of service, which meant the climb would take six hours as opposed to five.

We set off with the guide in the lead. The first bit beside the chair lift was easy, but after an hour or so we were scrambling up broken lava which, alternating with a glacier, was to be the pattern of the rest of the climb. All signs of vegetation had by this stage disappeared with nothing but ice, snow and evil looking black lava and pumice. At one stage we had to don crampons on the glacier. Fortunately these fitted over my trainers, and once used to them, I felt confident climbing steep inclines. However at this stage the Spanish boys, pleading exhaustion and vertigo, begged the guide to call a rescue helicopter! The guide spent some twenty minutes on his radio, before announcing that there could be no helicopter. Somehow the Spaniards were persuaded to keep going, albeit at a painfully slow pace. Finally at 3.45 p.m. and over six hours after leaving, we reached the lip of the summit crater, which was some quarter mile in diameter. Peering down several thousand feet we could see bright red molten rock. There was a strong stench of sulphur, which not only irritated our eyes and nose, but was a deterrent from lingering long looking down over the lip. Small puffs of steam were constantly emerging from the rocks just below this lip. Looking out east towards Argentina, we could see two more volcanoes, one of which was considerably higher than our 10,000 feet.

The climb down was rather quicker but tedious, because I could not enter the conversation. We were however back at the hotel before 9 p.m., well in time for Latin American drinks and dinner. We went out to a party with friends of Sebastian and his wife Victoria, and I was something of a hero. None of the Chileans present had climbed the volcano. Some weeks after we left, Sebastian sent me a cutting from the local paper, relating the tragedy of a guide taking a party of 'Ingleses' up the volcano. He had fallen down a crevasse on the glacier and perished. It was obviously hazardous to climb Villarica, so I was fortunate. I hope it was not our guide but he was probably alright as he didn't speak English!

We went on from Chile through Santiago to Guyaquil in Ecuador on the Pacific Coast, from where our plane was due to go the next day to the Galapagos. In Guyaquil we found a Panama hat shop. The best Panamas are made in Ecuador. Hats from $10 to $500 were on sale in a shop laid out in a similar manner to Lock's in St James. Alan and I each invested in both a smart $100 hat, and a cheaper version for the sun of the Galapagos, while Sarah and Tara bought ladies' sun hats.

It is a 100-minute flight out over the Pacific to the Galapagos Islands which were made famous by the visit of Charles Darwin and the *Beagle* in the 19th century. They are a fascinating collection of volcanic islands with unique flora and fauna, from brilliantly coloured crabs, through iguanas, to some fifteen varieties of finches found nowhere else in the world. Probably the most famous of the fauna are the giant turtles and the blue booby birds. What was so enthralling was how totally unfazed by humans all the native species were. This makes a visit to the Galapagos a must. However do go on a reasonably sized vessel (ours had 40 cabins) and ensure there are good guides.

Dick Carlsberg who had introduced me to YPO and invited me to his '3-Shot Honker Hunt' in 1982, in 1990 gave me one of my more thrilling experiences, when he took me elk hunting. At that time he owned a spectacular lodge, 'Brookes Lake' on the edge of the Teeton National Park in Wyoming. From there we set out on horseback, to ride some six hours to our camp in the national park, which is part of America's so called 'Wilderness Country'. In the wilderness country, nothing mechanical is allowed. The only way in is on foot or on horseback. Even power saws are banned, although the camp was allowed an electric generator.

We arrived at the camp shortly before dark. Having fed and watered our horses, we enjoyed a campfire barbecue, before turning in for a far from comfortable night in a tent. Next day, well before dawn, we were up and after saddling our horses, we rode up through so called 'meadows' – grassy patches on the edge of the forest – in the hope we would see or hear an elk as they usually came out to feed at dawn. However we had no luck, and rode on up eventually reaching 13000 feet in the Rockies. It was a crystal clear day, and even at 13000 feet remarkably warm. Having seen nothing, we rested up for some hours. There was no sign of life, except in the far distance, where we saw some wild sheep. At about 4 p.m. we set off to ride back, and at 7 p.m. with darkness drawing in, my guide heard the whistling of a male elk. They make a whistling noise in the rut, as opposed to the roar of a red deer stag. At the time we were riding along the edge of a 'meadow' next to the forest. My guide leapt off his horse, grabbed the rifle – a Weatherby 300 – from its holder, and crept off into the forest with me following. On hearing the elk whistle again, my guide produced a whistle himself, which the elk mistook for a rival and some ten minutes later he appeared some 70 yards away, a huge beast about three times the size of a stag, but with the same shape of horn. I shot him, without lying down, direct from the shoulder. I am glad to say it was a clean shot. By this time darkness was closing in, so having butchered the elk, we left him for the night. We had a further three hour ride in pitch dark back to camp. Fortunately horses have much better night vision than humans, and I just dropped the reins and let my horse follow the guides, in the meantime listening to horrific tales of grizzly bear encounters, and expecting one to spring out at any moment. (Ironically that day some ten miles away another hunter had been severely mauled, barely escaping with his life!)

We arrived back at camp around midnight, and again had an early start next day, when we rode up with three pack horses, onto which various parts of the elk were loaded. There followed a further eight hour ride back to the lodge. I really felt I had earned my elk, whose horns now adorn the 'shoot room' at my family's farm near Chester-le-Street. I also enjoyed the meat, which is a real delicacy. No one can sell native deer meat in the States, which eliminates any commercial reward from poaching.

I had been able to try and shoot an elk because Sarah and I were attending a YPO international meeting at Jacksonhole Wyoming. Wyoming, which we have also visited in winter for skiing, is a wild and sparsely populated state, with some large cattle stations and the famous Yellowstone National Park. Besides elk and deer hunting it has excellent trout fishing. I took some others back to Brookes Lake during the YPO meeting, where we did not have much luck actually fishing, but saw at close range a moose as well as some beaver.

In the nineties we attended a number of YPO International events. They were all memorable. Among those which stick particularly in our memory was the event in Argentina and Chile in 1993 where we heard addresses from the Presidents of Argentina, Uruguay, Paraguay and Chile in four days and then had a fascinating cruise around the Beagle Channel. Another meeting we attended was in Malaysia in 1996, organized by a son of the then King. We were addressed by the Deputy Prime Minister of the time, Amar Ibrahim, who, poor chap, subsequently went to prison having fallen out with Dr Mahathier. I found myself sitting next to the king at a dinner. He had his chief of police on the other side and conversation was not easy, although he had great charm. The one topic that really amused him was the story of the newspaper headline in the Sun about the then leader of the Liberal Party headed Paddy Pantsdown!

We have been to such politically incorrect places as Myanmar. The military dictatorship were keen to impress us. They claimed that to give up control would lead to civil war. We were taken to witness a huge ceremonial bonfire of drugs which they alleged was part of their policy to destroy the drug trade. Surprisingly they allowed a delegation from the group to meet Aung San Su Kyi. She is ethereally beautiful and it is easy to see why she is so revered in the western press, but politically she is very inflexible. She is no Mandela and I am far from certain that all the wrong is on the general's side. She greeted us with 'You should not have come to my country', when we said we had come to look and some might invest, bringing jobs, her response was 'We do not want your jobs, they are only for servants'! Burma is a beautiful country. No doubt the regime is highly illiberal, but I cannot help reflecting that we accept far greater human rights abuses in China because we don't want to offend them, but we can be beastly to the Burmese because they cannot bite back!

I also attended as a result of my membership of YPO and CEO, two Harvard Business School Seminars. The first in 1988 profoundly influenced the way I ran Vaux, particularly emphasizing delegation to, and empowerment of, those working for the company. It led to my shifting much of my chief executive's role in 1992 to two divisions, one run by Peter Catesby on the snooze side and the other by Frank Nicholson on the booze side. With hindsight I wish I had paid more attention to one of the major subjects covered – succession planning.

It was a very sad moment for Sarah and myself when we learnt, while we were attending an International Chapter meeting in San Francisco in August 1994, that Dick Carlsberg who had introduced us to YPO had collapsed and died while out grouse shooting on a property close to our own in Scotland. But for that chance dinner placing back in 1977 it is unlikely he would have been in Scotland or Sarah and I in San Francisco some 17 years later.

Sarah and I have made many YPO friends. I have previously mentioned Bill Tilley. Others include Riprand Arco, a German Count married to a member of the Hapsburg family, whom I first met at a Harvard Seminar in 1988 and introduced to the International Chapter. We have been his guests in both Austria and Germany where he has an interesting pheasant shoot. At the end of the day all the birds are laid out in a square, while candles are lit around them so that their spirits can escape skywards, presumably to heaven!

Particular friends are Chirayu and Malika Amin. He is a pharmaceutical king in India and a 'Mr Big'. In 1998 we had special cause to be grateful to him when with Angus and Gay Grossart and our respective daughters – a party of six – we had gone to India for Christmas and on 23rd December were due to fly to Trivandrum in South India from Bombay. At the airport we were told that we only had four confirmed tickets despite all our coupons looking in order. Having blown every possible fuse to no avail against the local bureaucracy, I rang Chirayu in desperation. He was some 400 miles away in Baroda. He told me not to worry. It would be sorted out and sure enough some 20 minutes later his representative appeared. All was fixed, two unfortunates were

1984, Winning the Royal Show Coaching Class.

obviously bumped off the plane and we were on our way! This is a classic example that what is important in life, is not what you know but who you know!

While YPO played a big part in social and personal life, it far from dominated. I had driven horses intermittently over the 15 years before I became Chairman of Vaux. After the Silver Jubilee I had decided to keep the Vaux coach team going and most years subsequently took it to Ascot continuing a unique form of corporate hospitality. I had first driven the coach at Ascot in the late sixties. Through the seventies my father usually took the coach on two days and I took it on one. We had as guests a mixture of personal and corporate friends. The horses were stabled originally at the Combermere barracks, but more recently, the Queen has allowed me and some senior members of the Coaching Club to stable for Ascot at the Windsor Castle Mews. On the days we go to the Races I drive the coach from the Mews through the Windsor Great Park, then up the back of the racecourse stands and into the far end of the paddock. We return the same way after the fifth race. The Coaching Club have a reserved area in the paddock where we give our guests a picnic lunch.

I also continued showing, and over the following years I drove the Vaux Team to victory at the Royal Show some six times,

1996, PDN President of the Coaching Club driving The Venture Coach in Newport, North Island to the team of Jack Seabrook, President of the New York Coaching Club.

equalling my father's record. As a result of my coaching, I was invited in 1987 to become Vice President of the Coaching Club succeeding Nigel Chamberlayne-MacDonald as President in 1990. The Coaching Club founded in 1871 is the oldest four-in-hand driving club in the world, being two years senior to the much smarter Coaching Club of New York.

In 1988 I was invited to judge the coaching classes at the Toronto Winter Fair, the premier horse show in North America. The American Coaching Club is very grand and Toronto is a dauntingly social occasion, requiring a white tie and tails every night. I wore this rig on eight of the ten nights I was there. The Coaching Judge sees the same teams of horses each night, but there is always a slight difference in what is required, so he is encouraged to spread the prizes around.

I had first met Jack Seabrook in 1966 and been over for his 70th birthday in 1987, by which time he had become President of the Coaching Club of New York. In 1992 Jack invited me in my capacity as President of the (English) Coaching Club, to attend the main meeting of the American Club which is held every two to four years in Newport, Rhode Island. At the same time his Vice President, Charles Matheson invited Sarah and me to stay for the meeting, in his mother-in-law's mansion on Bellevue Avenue. Newport was where the super rich of the late 19th and early 20th centuries built their 'cottages'. These are in fact virtually palaces, and the smartest of these are on Bellevue Avenue. An American is reputed to have asked a French aristocrat visiting Newport whether in France there were similar properties. The Frenchman's reply was 'Yes but not all on the same street!'

While Newport's main claim to fame is as headquarters of the New York Yacht Club, it is still a pinnacle of high society and 'old money'. Vanderbilt descendants still occupy a 'cottage' or two, although these are now largely owned by a preservation trust. As in Toronto, it is a sartorial challenge to spend four days in Newport requiring white tie, black tie, black top hat, grey top hat and morning (Coaching Club) coat. Each day there is a lunch party and again an evening party with at least one drive. Jack had a spare team of horses which he invited me to drive, so to help out I brought over my head coachman Tommy Greenlay, who had never crossed the Atlantic before. Sarah and I had flown over earlier to Boston and spent a few days in Maine, the northernmost and most attractive State of the United States Eastern seaboard, before heading into Newport's hectic social whirl.

We were asked back again in 1996 by which time we were feted even more richly, possibly because of the title! We stayed that time with David and Linda Lindh, secretary of the New York Coaching Club. He is a delightful friend, who has come to visit us several times in December, when he flies over in order to earn for himself enough air miles, so that he and his wife can commute in greater comfort between their homes in Texas and Newport. We returned again to Newport in 1999 at the conclusion of our world tour. A kind friend took my top hats etc over on that occasion, so that we did not have to take them around the world with us. We had also in 1997 been at Jack Seabrook's 80th birthday party held in Aiken,

South Carolina, a centre of carriage driving and foxhunting for the Southern United States. There we stayed with Lou Piancone, a remarkable Italian American member of the Coaching Club in the food supply business. The actual birthday party was a splendid dance in the grounds of a grand mansion house, but Lou had a lunch party next day, memorable both for the company and also the profusion of caviar.

That autumn I again was invited to judge the Toronto Winter Fair. But oh, the hazards of being a judge! Lou Piancone was showing, and he probably had the second nicest team overall there, however they did not go well all the time, particularly on a night when I had expected I would be able to put them first. He wrote me a letter damning my judging to which I made a diplomatic reply, but felt I had to show his letter elsewhere. It became political when I received letters praising my judging! All ended peacefully with an apology, but it was a lesson that as a judge one cannot win!

Coaching was an important part of my life in the nineties, particularly in my final year as President in 1996 when the Club made a 75th Birthday Presentation to Prince Philip, himself a driving member of the Club.

Among the advantages of no longer being Executive is that I have more time for shooting. County Durham has some of the finest grouse moors and pheasant shoots. Our family pheasant shoot at 'Southill' provides some testing high birds. It is not however quite on a par with 'Lambton' some three miles down the River Wear. This has been since the early 20th Century one of the great pheasant shoots. I have been asked there for the past 15 years. Lord Lambton the owner was in his heyday renowned to be the best shot in England and he gives his guests an unforgettable experience, not just shooting, but the extras such as Latour Claret for 'elevenses' and a magnificent feast for lunch.

Sarah and I also have a lot more time to travel. While no longer a young president, indeed no longer any sort of 'President' in the business sense of being a chief executive, Sarah and I since I left Vaux have been with our friends in the International Chapter of the Young Presidents to several exotic locations including Mexico, where we were particularly impressed by a speech to us by the then opposition Presidential candidate, now President, Vicente Fox.

In 2001 we were in Cuba where we had Castro to dinner one night, when he turned up in his combat fatigues. He then invited us all (some 100 of us) back to dinner with him. We had to cancel our other arrangements but were then lavishly entertained by him (this time in a suit). Fortunately we did not have to endure a long oration. His speech was very short for him (only 20 minutes) and quite humorous, although the jokes came through an interpreter as it was in Spanish. All the men were presented with a box of his special 'El Trinidad' cigars and a packet of pep pills rumoured to be the Cuban equivalent of Viagra, while the ladies were given scent. Castro has an imposing presence and charisma but it is a dreadful regime. Everyone has a wage of $20 per month plus food stamps. No one can own a house. People live in the accommodation they are allocated. No-one can buy a car of later than 1959 vintage, so what cars there are other than those of the regime apparatchiks, are magnificent ancient Chevrolets, Buicks and Cadillacs etc., the ultimate Gas Guzzlers. On the other hand literacy is virtually 100%, and there are more trained doctors per head of population than in any other country on earth. Old Havana has been carefully restored and is stunning. Castro replaced in 1959 a thoroughly corrupt regime, the exiles of which are a powerful political voice in Miami. Their support for President Bush probably tipped the election his way in 2000.

It is rumoured that Castro is not in the best of health, and I would expect his regime will not long survive his demise.

In 2002 we were in Taiwan followed by Shanghai and Beijing. It is staggering to see the development going on in Shanghai and Beijing. We did not meet any high ups in Taiwan because they disapproved of us going on to China, nor in China because we had been in Taiwan! However Shanghai is an extraordinarily vibrant city. The famous Bund has been painstakingly restored including the Peace Hotel built by the Sassoons in the 1920s. We stayed on the other side of the river on the 80th floor of the recently opened Grand Hyatt Hotel. Unfortunately the weather was poor while we were there and at our height we were in the clouds, which possibly prevented vertigo on looking out.

I had a mental picture of Beijing as consisting of wide boulevards full of bicycles. The reality is that the boulevards are there, but the bicycles are few in number and the traffic very heavy, the signs of a prosperous city. In Beijing we were taken to the University to meet bright and westernized students. They had full access to the internet and a profound wish to have the benefits of the West. It is still however a politically nasty society. Almost all the students were only children because of the draconian one child law. In the longer term this will lead to serious problems, but China is an awakening economic giant with great entrepreneurial drive. With its huge population, it may become as powerful as the United States in the next 30 years.

CHAPTER 7

Public Life

I HAVE BEEN FORTUNATE to have had the opportunity to play some part in the regeneration of the North East in the eighties and nineties.

Some of the fall-out from the Thatcher reforms were painful for the North East. Having become involved in the wider region as a result of my Chairmanship of the Regional CBI from 1977 to 1979, I was keen to continue a role in the region believing, I hope not too conceitedly, that I was in a position to make a contribution. Anything that could be done to help the region recover had a major spin off for Vaux, which was dependent for much of its success on increasing prosperity among its heartland customers. I was flattered to be invited to chair a subsidiary of the state owned British Technology Group (BTG) aiming to provide finance for small and medium size business in the North East. The concept of Venture Capital was at the time in its infancy. 3i's, or Investors in Industry as they were then known, were in existence, owned at the time by the big clearing banks, but both they and BTG had not at the time really taken on board that their role was not to provide soft money for doubtful ventures, but to make money by backing potentially successful operations.

I was lucky to acquire a strong chief executive, Michael Denny. In 1985 along with him, I arranged a privatization into Northern Investors ltd with funds which I helped to raise from leading companies and local authorities within the region. We recruited a good board of mainly regional businessmen. Northern Investors was subsequently floated and investors who have stuck with the company have seen their investment grow several fold. I chaired the new company until 1989 when I handed over to Robert Dickinson. Michael Denny and his team subsequently formed their own management company Northern Ventures which now manage a number of other funds.

The eighties were an exciting time personally. I served my year as High Sheriff of Durham back in 1980. This was at a time when I was very involved in initiatives at Vaux and in a bid for the North East TV franchise. Fortunately the post of High Sheriff, which has a longer history than that of Lord Lieutenant, was less onerous then than it has subsequently become. There was no Shrievality Association to invent slightly bogus rituals and create not very productive work. The main function was to entertain judges in the region including such as Mr Justice Taylor, subsequently Lord Chief Justice who came from the North East. I remember particularly, Mr Justice Caulfield of fragrant Mary Archer fame. He was a most charming, if rather sad man, after the collapse of his marriage. All the judges, who at that time had lodgings at Meadomsley in the North and Kirk Levington in the South, were good company to entertain. Few stood on ceremony, although there was one occasion after dinner had been announced, when the judge and the then Lord Lieutenant collided in the doorway as each sought to establish precedence. The highlight of the Durham Sheriff's year is the service for the Courts in the Cathedral held in July. The High Sheriff traditionally gives a lunch after this service for the legal profession. I broke with tradition in not holding this lunch in Durham Castle, and followed my predecessor's example in holding it at home. It was hosted in Sarah's name. The guests were drawn from the wider community and not just the legal profession, which meant some of the lesser legal luminaries could not be accommodated and went hungry. This was not very popular! At the end of my year as Sheriff I was appointed a Deputy Lieutenant of the County.

Vaux had been a founder member of the Northern Industrialists Protection Association (NIPA). This was set up during the post-war Labour Government by Northern Industrialists to combat the threats of socialism particularly at that time nationalization. It had had a resurgence in the late 1970s when the policies of a Labour Government were again perceived as hostile to industry. The

1980, PDN High Sheriff with Sheriff's Chaplain Alan Chesters, subsequently Bishop of Blackburn and Judge Mr Justice Smith.

organization raised substantial funds from North East Industry for political purposes, mainly, but not exclusively, for support of the Conservative party. Financial help was also occasionally given to other anti socialist parties including Liberals.

When my father retired, I took his place on the NIPA Council then Chaired by Sir James Woodeson, Chairman of Northern Engineering Industries. Jimmy Woodeson was a considerable character and the architect of the creation of what was then the North East's largest company with the merger of Reyrolle's and Parsons. He and Sir John Hunter of Swan Hunter were the North East's leading businessmen of the 1970s.

When Jimmy was tragically killed in a motor smash, I was elected his successor as Chairman in 1981. This gave me an entrée to the Conservative Government.

During the seventies, Sarah and I had become great friends of David and Mary Coltman and through them I met her father then the Rt Hon William Whitelaw MP, Deputy Leader of the

Conservative Party. Sarah had also known him before we were married as one of her great friends was another daughter, Carol Whitelaw, who is also our daughter Lucy's Godmother.

He liked to be addressed as Willie by young and old alike. He was one of the shrewdest and nicest of men. He had the ability to make me and others feel when talking to him that we were very special and that he really wanted to hear what we had to say. His contribution to British life, particularly in tempering the genius of Margaret Thatcher through the eighties, was unique.

I had several meetings with him when he was in government and afterwards. Some were at my request, to seek his advice on how to handle such issues as the privatization of the North East subsidiary of the British Technology Group into Northern Investors, and more importantly, to explain the thinking behind the Northern Development Company. Others were at his request when he sought my views on Northern issues. Until his move to the House of Lords, he had been MP for Penrith. At the time, Cumbria was more part of the North East than North West, looking to Newcastle rather than Manchester. Willie was very committed to helping the region. Even after he retired from politics, he did a lot of work in the region, particularly in helping raise funds for Durham University where he involved me.

I caused a number of eyebrows to be raised in Boodle's dining room when I took the great man to lunch there before Nicholas Ridley's funeral. I could see people thinking how was I on such terms!

In the early eighties, while there was a general feeling that if we were to get anywhere as a region we had to do it ourselves, there were elements in the local media and among local politicians who were continually whingeing about the problems. It was the then Prime Minister, Margaret Thatcher, who galvanized some of us to take action. She came up and while it is doubtful she ever actually made remarks about 'Moaning Minnies' directly in relation to the North East, nevertheless there was a clear message coming out that this was how we were perceived.

Sir Ralph Carr-Ellison took the initiative to commission a

consultants' report prepared by Miles Middleton of Coopers, the accountants. This was funded after a whip-round among local industrialists. The report produced a recommendation that what was needed was a body made up of industry, local government and organized labour to co-ordinate inward investment. Many of us looked with envy north of the border at the Scottish Development Agency, which was heavily subsidized by the taxpayer and was able to offer very favourable terms to potential investors. It was also able to co-ordinate infrastructure developments which were effectively tackling many of the structural problems of the Scottish economy. It was made clear to us that we could not expect this level of support, but that for inward investment there were funds available if we could get our act together. At that stage there was a co-ordinating body called the North East Development Corporation (NEDC) which had some 35 members, of whom around 90% were councillors. This body had fallen into disrepute with tales of extravagant entertaining hitting the media. The 'Cooper Report' suggested a much more focussed body with equal representation from the three parties, employers, unions and local government. I joined a Steering Group led by Councillor Hugh Little of Cumbria, a far sighted man who was widely respected in local government.

After many meetings, mainly held at the week-end, spent thrashing out a constitution all parties could sign up to, the idea of an inward investment company emerged. This would be part nationally funded and part funded locally by industry and councils. It was agreed that there would be a board of eleven members – five from local government, three from industry and three from unions, with an independent chairman, and that it would be called the 'Northern Development Company'. It was essential however, that the new body, if it was to work, needed the blessing of central government. At that stage, certain elements of the local Tory party who had not been involved tried to persuade ministers not to give that support to what they seemed to think, was a socialist front organization. I was fortunately able to intervene, and keep progress towards such a company from

1985, Picture from article in Northern Business *taken in front of Quarry Hill (reproduced by courtesy of* The Journal*).*

stalling. The company was set up in 1986. During the next 11 years, under the successive Chairmanships of Reay Atkinson, Ron Dearing and George Russell, it became the most effective body in Britain at securing and maintaining inward investment in the regions and at a fraction of the cost of achieving the same objective in Scotland.

While most of the funding came from central government, my private sector colleagues on the board and I were able to secure the support of the private sector to the tune of several hundred thousand pounds a year in cash and kind. The local authorities also made a major contribution.

The secret behind the success of the Northern Development Company was that industry, unions and local government really felt they owned the Company. Everyone pulled in the same direction.

After an initial hiccough, we recruited an excellent Chief Executive, Dr John Bridge, who led the Company for most of its existence, and we were particularly fortunate in our chairmen. We chose them. They were not government appointees but each was a man of weight and authority.

Our first Chairman, Reay Atkinson CB, had been Regional Director of the DTI for the region, a position he had filled with considerable distinction, being largely responsible for bringing the Nissan car plant to the North East.

When he retired we appointed a panel to find a successor on which I took the lead and were able to recruit Sir Ron (later Lord) Dearing. He had come to know the region in the seventies when he too had been a Regional Director of the DTI. He had then gone on to run the Post Office and in the late eighties was the principal government trouble-shooter. 'Send for Lord Dearing' became the cry when ministers faced seemingly intractable problems in a number of fields, particularly education. In spite of his numerous other commitments he gave an enormous amount of time and energy to the company. When he went, we again were fortunate to find another real heavyweight to chair us in the shape of Sir George Russell, a native of the North East who had made his career in aluminium. He also chaired the Independent Broadcasting Authority and later 3i's. Each Chairman had the necessary diplomatic skills to keep the disparate elements together.

The company would not have worked if any of the three major elements had fallen out. Towards the end of its existence, certain newer directors from the Local Government side tried to call a vote, but when they realized that such a move by local government trying to throw its weight around might drive out the private sector, they fortunately withdrew.

Each of the constituencies appointed its own directors but while there was a regional organization to make these appointments for local government and the unions, there was none for the private sector until the establishment in 1994 of the Northern Business Forum. Sir Ian Wrigglesworth and I set this up drawing members from the regional and local business bodies, particularly the Chambers of Commerce and the CBI. However there was no controversy about who was selected and voted in as private sector directors by the individual companies who made up the private sector memberships.

The incoming Labour Government in 1997 had included in its manifesto a commitment to regional development agencies. In the North East, the NDC was able to form the nucleus of the new development agency 'One North East', where John Bridge became Chairman. One North East has a much wider remit than NDC, however the board for this agency is appointed by central government and is a 'top down' operation. The jury is out on how effective it will prove to be.

My main contribution to public life in the North East was my Chairmanship of the Tyne & Wear Development Corporation, throughout its existence. In 1986 the government announced its intention of setting up four new development corporations, based on a model established by Michael Heseltine, when he set up the London Docklands Development Corporation, to be followed by a similar corporation on Merseyside. The idea was to select a limited area suffering severe economic decline, and then establish a body to redevelop that area, giving it planning powers and funding, with the aim of creating an environment into which substantial private sector investment would be drawn. The intention was that Urban Development Corporations would become beacons within the region they operated, and there would be a knock on effect throughout a much wider area.

Our Urban Development Area (UDA) covered 20 miles of riverbanks on the Tyne and the Wear and some 6,000 acres. When we started there were still shipyards on the Wear and working collieries on both rivers none of which were anticipated to go in the near future. Their demise compounded our problems. In my first year I had taken the opportunity to visit urban regeneration projects in Toronto, Boston and Baltimore. It was interesting that the regeneration projects in both Boston and Baltimore had been going 30 years and were still far from complete. I believe we achieved as much or more in our 10 years.

When Nicholas Ridley, then Secretary of State for the Environment, interviewed me for appointment I told him that I did not believe the Corporation should have an indefinite life and that about 10 years was the appropriate time. We did not want to be in the same position as many of the new towns which ran out of steam. A finite life was a spur to achievement. I was appointed in January 1987 and the corporation was established on the first of May that year. We had one outstanding candidate for the position of Chief Executive in Alastair Balls, then Northern Director of the Department of the Environment. Alastair is the finest public servant I have met, combining vision and entrepreneurial flair but always acting selflessly. If he had operated in the private sector he could have achieved much greater material reward. We are fortunate in this country, still to have very able men prepared to serve the community or their country in the civil and indeed foreign and armed services, for limited reward.

I also was able to help select a board from local business, the trade unions and local government who were totally committed to the corporation. If I can boast of anything, it is that apart from isolated planning matters, the board always achieved unanimity, although not without lively debate and argument.

From the start the board were determined to work with local government and representatives of the community. It was not always easy. We operated in four district authorities, Sunderland, South Tyneside, North Tyneside and Newcastle. There was a natural resentment that we had, in effect, usurped some of these authorities' planning powers, and had access to substantial funding not available to them. Some accused us of being undemocratic, to which my reply was, we were responsible to central government, and through them to the country and the taxpayer. While local or regional democracy may be desirable in many circumstances, in the end it is the democratically elected national government that has the big picture, and responsibility for allocating national resource raised from taxpayers.

However, we were always aware that, in order to achieve substantial development that made a positive contribution to the quality of life, we had to find means whereby the people affected by our developments really had ownership of them. I believe we were unique among Urban Development Corporations in many of our initiatives, such as monitoring panels, and access and education support. The developments we have undertaken are flourishing and have achieved a momentum now extended to areas we were not able to complete during our lifetime.

The raw statistics show that we spent some £450 million or just over £40 million a year of taxpayers' money, we generated £1.3 billion of private sector investment and were responsible for some 38,000 jobs.

At an early stage after our formation, I took our board on a river cruise up both the Tyne and the Wear, and while this did not give exactly a bird's eye view of the vast amounts of dereliction, it did bring home the magnitude of the task. The Government had commissioned a report from consultants before setting up the corporation and this had identified some of the worst problems although ironically completely overlooking one of them, the Hawthorn Leslie Yard which was to be transformed into the St Peters Basin development in Newcastle.

It was not always smooth going. We had significant run ins with

'Brewing Thoroughbred', cartoon illustrating article in Northern Echo, *17 May 1993 (reproduced courtesy of the* Northen Echo*).*

two Members of Parliament, one of whom is now a prominent government minister. It is a hazard of public life that there are always those quick to make unfounded allegations of wrongdoing, if one does not agree with them. We had our share of such.

Of our original board of ten, four others served through the life of the corporation. I was particularly fortunate to have John Ward as my deputy. At the start he was still Regional Director of Barclays Bank, but also involved in a number of North East companies. John is a very able man and carries great respect on Tyneside. The others who served throughout were Ralph Iley, a combination of shrewd businessman and doyen of the pigeon-racing world, John Barnsley, a senior partner in Price Waterhouse and Joe Mills of the Transport Union whom I respected enormously from the days of the Norseman TV challenge. It is a tragedy for the region that Joe died in January 2003 after a long battle with cancer. He had an infectious sense of humour but more importantly he was a highly intelligent and articulate champion of the North East who in the seventies and eighties was far-sighted enough to bring about a major rapprochement between unions and employers in the region. This made the North East attractive for new investment.

Most important however, to the success of the project was the quality of local government representation from Sep Robinson of South Shields and John Donnelly of Sunderland in the early days through Eric Bramfitt, Bryn Siddaway and especially Tony Flynn who became leader of Newcastle Council. We always had a representative from local authority opposition parties, initially this was Bert Moore, then latterly Ian Gordon, but this never produced friction. Others who served in the initial stages were Sir John Hall, of Metro fame, and Graeme Anderson, former deputy chairman of Northern Engineering. In the latter stages we had Professor Patsy Healey of the Centre for Research in Urban Environment and Jane Darbyshire, a lively and challenging specialist in design, also Ian (now Sir Ian) Gibson of Nissan and Frank Sharratt, Chairman of Kerr McGee Oil, a remarkable businessman who looks more like a professor and was largely responsible for the success of the Bede's World museum project.

One board member Chris Sharpe served for only three years before sadly dying of a heart attack. He was Chief Executive of Northern Rock at the time, and largely responsible for laying the groundwork of that company's success.

My part was similar to that of a non-executive Chairman in a private company. I represented the Corporation to the outside world, dealing with a succession of ministers following Nicholas Ridley, including Tony Newton, Michael Portillo and John Redwood.

Of these Michael Portillo was the most sympathetic while John Redwood was the hardest taskmaster, although none could compare with Margaret Thatcher who visited the corporation once. She had come up primarily to be principal guest at the 'North East Businessman of the Year' Dinner sponsored by Vaux Group's Swallow Hotels subsidiary and the *Journal* newspaper. Having sat next to her that evening, I then accompanied her the

1989, Speaking at the NE Businessman of the Year Awards with principal guest, The Rt Hon Margaret Thatcher (photo courtesy of The Journal*).*

next day for a fraught morning, endeavouring to answer a series of penetrating questions. I had always learnt from army days that one should never admit to not knowing the answer, but it was unnerving that Margaret Thatcher would correct my answers. She was far better briefed than I was!

John Redwood took an active interest in board appointments, at one stage seeking to override my strong recommendation. However when I said I would have to resign if he persisted, he fortunately gave way gracefully.

One of the more pleasant duties I had was to help persuade companies from overseas to relocate with us or at least in the region. Attracting investment from the Far East was a critical aim, not just for the Urban Development Corporation, but also for the Northern Development Company. I made visits for this purpose to Korea, Taiwan, Japan (three times) and Hong Kong. In the Far East 'face' is very important. To have supposedly 'top people' visiting prospects for inward investment is an important part of the marketing strategy.

Korea's progress since the war 50 years ago has taken that country from the gross domestic product level of Tanzania to one of the world's most dynamic economies. They are still on a semi war footing with the communist North and a visit to the 38th parallel reveals old style frontier fortifications now unique since the collapse of the East German Regime. While there are some signs at the present time of a thaw in relations, there is still no peace treaty.

I cannot say I appreciated Korean cuisine, although Taiwan was a different matter. We were taken on one trip around the kitchen of the Hyatt Regency Hotel in Taipei. As an hotelier in my commercial life I was staggered by the sophistication of this operation.

I enjoyed something of an Annus Mirabilis in 1992. The Vaux horses had swept all before them with me driving them to victory in three 'Royal' shows – Windsor, the 'Royal' itself and The Highland Show, while my brother Frank was the 'whip' when they also won the Great Yorkshire. At the end of that year I received a letter from 10 Downing Street, asking for my agreement for my name to be put forward for a Knighthood 'for services to industry and the public in North East England'. This was the greatest thrill of my career.

In June 1992 the Development Corporation had sponsored a concert tour by the Northern Symphonia Orchestra to Japan. In May that year, we learnt that the Crown Prince was to attend one of the concerts and it was more or less instructed that Sarah and myself should be present for this occasion. It was not a very convenient time, particularly as it disrupted long laid plans for driving my horses at Ascot. However off we went.

It was a successful evening although I think the Crown Prince was as bemused as I was by a piece by Schnitke, which sounded more like a cacophony of dentists' drills. The Japanese Royal Family have even stricter protocol than our own.

As we were in Japan I hosted other receptions for concerts in

1993, Investiture with Sarah and Lucy.

Osaka and Nagoya and made several courtesy calls on inward investors. Sarah and I also managed to fit in a visit to Kyoto where we stayed the night at a Japanese 'Ryokan'. This was an interesting experience. I believe it is even more interesting for unaccompanied gentlemen! On arrival, great ceremony is made of removing shoes, and then being escorted to a room with a picture window onto a tiny garden. The ambience is meant to create serenity. In the room there was a low table but no sign of a bed. The bathroom had a wooden tub, which the female attendant proceeded to fill before discreetly retiring to leave Sarah and me to our ablutions. We had been warned that the most cardinal sin in such a situation is to use soap in the bath. There were small towels and a drain hole in the floor where we scrubbed ourselves down. If a man is on his own, I understand this is a service performed by the female attendant!

Afterwards we were invited to sit on cushions before the low table on which a Japanese meal was laid out. Then the attendant produced bedding rolls to make up our 'Futon' in which we passed a not very comfortable night. Next morning after breakfast came the shock of the bill, some £700! When we eventually exited we found that our shoes had not even been cleaned. It was a contrast to our Tokyo Hotel the 'Seijo Ginza', quite one of the best hotels we ever stayed in and half the price of the Ryokan.

The other memorable event of this trip was meeting a Mr Ishibashi. Mr Ishibashi of the Bridgestone Tyre Company was a great expert on Pointer dogs and I was given an introduction by a friend in that world, Anthony Scott-Harden. Mr Ishibashi offered to meet us on our return from Osaka and his office were anxious to know exactly which carriage we were in on the bullet train. When we arrived we learnt why. There was a delegation as we stepped out, consisting of Mr Ishibashi and a lady from the McCormach public relations organization. After the necessary introductions with lots of bowing, Mr Ishibashi invited us to the Ishibashi Museum. However we were not to travel with him but with the lady from McCormach who during the course of the journey explained about Mr Ishibashi. Apparently a prominent member of the Royal Family had sought his daughter's hand in marriage but Mr Ishibashi had said No. Japanese aristocracy had lost their actual titles after the war, but Mr Ishibashi was clearly one of them. The Ishibashi Museum had one of the world's leading exhibitions of impressionist art alongside another of ancient Egyptian artefacts and was quite fascinating even to a philistine like me.

The Ishibashis were charming hosts at a dinner that night, and we count ourselves fortunate to have seen a side of Japan that hardly exists. We did not see his home in central Tokyo which apparently has a large garden and air-conditioned kennels for his Pointers. He also told us about his own golf course, and showed us pictures of him dressed in what appeared to be the uniform of a Shogun.

This was one of four visits I made to Japan. The first was in 1979 when I tried to interest them in our Scottish beer. The others were for the Development Corporation in 1988, 1992 and 1996. It is an inscrutable country, very difficult to get around without a guide. It was always disconcerting, when holding meetings with companies, to be confronted by a delegation on the other side, whose size depended on the importance of the principal executive attending. Each meeting was preceded by an elaborate ceremony of exchanging cards. These cards are printed in English on one side and Japanese on the other. The correct way is to hand each one out in order of seniority, always presenting it with two hands and a bow with the Japanese side uppermost so that the recipient can read the donor's name. Meetings were full of pleasantries and it was only much later that one learnt whether anything would come of it.

In contrast both Korea and particularly Taiwan were more Western in their approach. A visit to Taiwan must include a visit to the main museum which contains a huge quantity of treasures taken from the mainland when the nationalist forces fled there in 1948. It was claimed, when I was there in 1993, that so numerous were these treasures, that even changing the exhibitions every three months, there were still items that had never been displayed. It is fortunate for the world that these treasures were removed as much of what was left in China was destroyed during the Cultural Revolution.

My favourite Far Eastern business destination however used to be Hong Kong. It had an even greater air of frenetic entrepreneurial activity than the United States. When I went back in 1997 after handover, I thought then nothing much had changed. I am afraid this is no longer true. We felt during our visit in 2002, that there was not the 'buzz' about the place that had made Hong Kong so exciting. On a personal level I used to get 'shirted, suited and shod' in Hong Kong for a fraction of UK prices, although in recent times the bargains have become less attractive and Bangkok represents better value. In 1996 one of our potential inward investors was in the bicycle manufacturing business with a plant just over the border in Red China. To visit him was comparatively easy. After crossing the border, we then drove through miles of construction projects over an area which must be one of the largest developments in the world. Eventually we reached the bicycle factory. It was highly efficient but health and safety considerations were non-existent, with open welding and no protection. The attitude to human life is still rather different!

The Corporation was due to end in 1998 under whichever party was in government. The wind down proceeded smoothly and I quote below my final Chairman's statement:

> When I agreed to be Chairman of the Tyne & Wear Development Corporation, I told the then Secretary of State that if we were to be effective and to succeed in the massive tasks we faced, we needed ten years to achieve long-term impact. Without a deadline I thought that it would be difficult to maintain the sense of urgency which was necessary if we were to make a real impact. While that task looked daunting in 1987, it became even more so with the closure of the shipyards and the remaining collieries at Westoe and Monkwearmouth, neither of which were foreseen when we started. We achieved what we set out to do in just ten years and ten months.
>
> So, what have we achieved? Apart from exceeding all the targets set for us by Government, we leave two riverbanks revitalized. 34,000 people work for companies which have either expanded or were not by the rivers before. Over 10,000 people live in the new communities we have created with the construction of 4,500 new homes. Where there was ruin and dereliction there are now attractive river walks, parks and leisure facilities and a new sense of purpose and prosperity.
>
> Of course, this has not been achieved by us alone and I would like to pay tribute to the co-operation we have received from our four local authorities as well as several other agencies and, of course, the private sector. It was not easy for local authorities to accept our presence which deprived them, during our time, of some of their powers and control over the areas in which we were operating but fortunately in the North East we have a tradition, born of the vicissitudes we have faced, of working together to achieve the best common result. We were always assiduous in our efforts to involve local people living nearby and most directly affected by what we were trying to do. Our community monitoring

panels were, I believe, unique among urban development corporations in enabling local people to have direct input and ownership of our plans. They insisted, rightly, on the highest standards in which they take a fierce pride.

The legacy we leave behind for coming generations is one of people and businesses, living and working in an environment fit for the new millennium. We have won many awards for our work – for the last year alone two top honours in the 1998 Civic Trust awards for the landscaping of the urban villages at Royal Quays and the architecture of Newcastle Central Riverside, as well as a Britain in Bloom national award for Sunderland.

We had a specific task and a short life. It has been an exciting time for all involved with the opportunity to bring new life to the region. Under a dynamic Chief Executive, Alastair Balls CB, a great team was put together to fulfil our vision. I was particularly proud to be Chairman of a board coming from different backgrounds which was always united in driving towards our objective, but at the same time, providing invaluable expertise and experience. We can all hold our heads high at the difference the Corporation has made to the region. Not only have we been an engine of irrevocable change, we have proved that in regeneration the North East can compete with the best in the world.

Besides the Development Company and Tyne Tees I was also a member of the North East Electricity Board (NEEB), before privatization and subsequently was a director of Northern Electric post privatization until it became the victim of a fierce takeover battle in 1997. I joined NEEB on the understanding that it was to be privatized.

Privatization of electricity creating a somewhat artificial division between generation and supply on one hand, and distribution on the other, has actually worked surprisingly well. Given that distribution is a natural monopoly, the introduction of a regulator has driven the industry to achieve far higher standards of productivity and service than might have been anticipated.

What in the long term is more worrying, is the degree to which our power supply and distribution is controlled by forces outside this country, resulting largely from the turmoil created by a succession of bids and deals. The first of these was from Trafalgar House for Northern Electric.

I was attending a meeting of the Brewers & Licensed Retailers Association of which I was then Chairman, when I received an urgent message to ring Nigel Rich an acquaintance whom I had met when he was 'Taipan' of Jardine Matheson in Hong Kong. I had not a clue as to what this could be about. When I rang him he told me he was Chief Executive of Trafalgar House, and having failed to contact the Chairman or Chief Executive of Northern Electric he was seeking through me, to inform the company that Trafalgar were about to announce a bid. I told him in fairly brusque terms that to approach a non-executive director was not the correct approach to a company, and that he must speak to the Chairman before such an announcement. This did delay the announcement in time for me to get a warning of what was happening to the Chairman. Trafalgar had been a successful building company but had been acquired by the Keswick Family's Jardine Matheson in what was to turn out to be a pretty disastrous attempt to diversify.

The logic behind the bid was non-existent, except that in a shrewd move Credit Suisse, Trafalgar's Advisor, had organized a 'contract for differences'. This worked by them acquiring options over Northern's shares. These were cashed after announcement of the bid which obviously had inflated Northern's price. It was a move of doubtful legality but it made enough to cover Trafalgar's costs of the bid. In Northern's case the cost of a successful defence was some £16 million, paid to our advisors Warburg's, and the lawyers. In typical fashion the only real beneficiaries of this piece of corporate drama were the corporate advisors on both sides.

From Northern's point of view, the price offered did not seem good value, but might have become so, after new rules from the electricity regulator were announced. These appeared to reduce the scope for profit. Upon this, in a previously unheard of move, Trafalgar and their advisors sort to 'gazunder' their bid and extend the time scale. The takeover panel who are supposed to police bids on a non legal basis, having changed the rules for contracts for differences after that horse had bolted, then stood their rules further on their head by saying that this bid could go ahead if authorized by shareholders in a general meeting. Up until that time, one of their firmest rules was that a failed bidder could not come back for a year, if he did not win within the laid down 60 day timetable.

A US arbitrageur named Weiser-Pratt gained sufficient support from institutions to force an EGM where fortunately he was soundly defeated. I accompanied the Chairman David Morris on rounds seeking support for Northern Electric before the EGM – Most institutions took our argument that this move breached the spirit and the letter of the takeover rules but certain major institutions sort a quick buck.

Trafalgar's move, which cost Northern some £16 million to defend, made them vulnerable to the next approach from 'Calen', an American based company. In a bitterly fought battle 'Calen' had not obtained sufficient acceptances to meet takeover panel rules that the bid must be concluded within 60 days of the offer. However as part of the defence, our advisors had bought shares without following the panel's procedure on disclosure. For this 'crime' the panel extended the offer period by some four days, which was enough for 'Calen' to win. In this case it was the shareholders of Northern who lost out, as almost certainly a higher price could have been achieved.

I had been convinced for a long time that takeover battles should only be conducted within a tightly defined legal framework. The 'panel' is a hopeless policing body which clever corporate advisors run rings around.

While that was the end of an independent Northern Electric the new American owners behaved reasonably generously initially, appointing Northern Electric Chairman David Morris and Neville Trotter to their board, but they quickly ceased to play any supporting role in the North East. This was in contrast to Northumbrian Water where the French owners have maintained a fine tradition of support for the community.

Shortly after the Northern Electric saga, Granada made an

agreed offer for Yorkshire Tyne Tees and I found myself lacking any other non-executive positions as I was planning to wind down my role at Vaux.

My last direct involvement in the commercial side of North East public life was in the new North East Chamber of Commerce resulting from a merger of the Tyne & Wear, Tynedale and Teesside Chambers into one body. I was approached in 1995 to be the inaugural President. I had not previously been involved with the Chamber movement, mainly because of ongoing connections with CBI nationally as well as regionally. The CBI basically covered big business and was a top down organization. The Chamber movement in contrast is a bottom up affair, and as a result had not developed into a regional voice for business. Historically in the North East there has been a certain amount of tribalism between different parts of the region particularly the Tyne and the Tees. It took farsighted leadership in these two areas to bring their respective chambers together. I guess I was approached as I came from Durham – somewhere in the middle! The aim of the new Chamber was to have a much more cohesive voice for business in the region.

At the time of the approach I was still Chairman of the Development Corporation, and also serving a two-year stint as Chairman of the National Brewers and Licensed Retailers Association, so it was not, from my point of view, ideal timing. However, the North East Chamber did get off the ground following a hectic 1995 New Year of extraordinary meetings of the previous Chambers to approve the merger. We were fortunate after a shaky start with a Chief Executive who was more suited to entrepreneurial activity than running a trade association, to recruit Michael Bird as Chief Executive. It went from strength to strength. He has recently retired, leaving behind a big success story.

My main charitable activities continue to be President of the Durham Association of Clubs for Young People, a post I have held since the early eighties, and more recently I was one of the instigators in setting up a Community Foundation called the

County Durham Foundation in 1995. I was its first Chairman handing this over in 2002. I am now its President.

Community Foundations originated in America. They are designed to enable people of modest means to make a significant and permanent contribution to the communities that live around them. The idea is to raise endowment capital funds, the income from which, after meeting the expenses of the foundation, is used for local causes. Donors to a foundation can play a greater or lesser part in how their funds are used. They can use Community Foundations as the vehicle to channel money to specific causes. They can have 'donor advised' funds where the Foundation consults them about how to use the money, or they can leave it to the trustees discretion. Gifts to foundations can be made by Companies or individuals either during their lifetime or by legacy.

In the early 1990s the Charles Stuart Mott Foundation of Cleveland Ohio decided to try and introduce the idea of foundations to the UK. They did this by seeking out groups of people interested in the idea, and then issuing a 'Challenge' that if these groups could raise £1 million they would match it. The three groups selected for the challenge were Bristol, Cleveland and Tyne & Wear. Vaux was a major contributor to the latter two who quickly met the challenge.

However, Durham lying between Cleveland and Tyne & Wear was left out.

My Predecessor as Lord Lieutenant, David Grant, set up a committee to try and form a foundation in Durham but this was proving difficult. I had previously been involved with a similar initiative set up by the Bishop of Durham for the Church Urban Fund and David Grant asked me to help.

I was able to use the experience Vaux had gained in this area, particularly as to who among regional companies could be approached for substantial help, while David used his local government connections to obtain support from the County Council and the District Authorities. This enabled us to launch the Foundation at a dinner held at Durham Cricket Ground with the then leader of the opposition Tony Blair as principal guest in

1999, With Mother and younger brother Frank at the High Sheriff Service for the Court.

July 1995. It was at this time looking very likely that Tony Blair would be the next Prime Minister, as these were the dying days of the Major government.

In spite of Durham being one of the poorest counties in Mainland Britain we now have endowment funds of over £3 million, but in addition we administer substantial 'flow through' funds for other agencies such as the Coalfields Regeneration Trust. The foundation under its dynamic director Gillian Stacey is a success. We started much later than our neighbouring foundations. It is a cause of some regret for us that before we came into existence, a Durham man left several million pounds to Tyne & Wear who are now the largest foundation in the country. There is also a problem with boundaries in that Cleveland County has been abolished and that part North of the Tees is now in Durham, however the Cleveland foundation is continuing. There is a slight awkwardness, in that as Lord Lieutenant of a County which now again extends to the Tees in the south east and indeed well south of the Tees in the west, I am only close to one of the two foundations operating within the county boundary. Fortunately however, there have not so far been serious friction or demarcation problems.

I was actually appointed Lord Lieutenant in January 1997. I succeeded David Grant who sadly died in 2002. The appointment is by the Queen on the recommendation of the Prime Minister (at that time John Major). There is a compulsory retirement date of one's 75th birthday, which in my case is 7th March 2013. It was with some hesitation that I accepted the position. I thought I might not have enough time for the job. I am now very glad that I did accept because, while interesting in its own right, it keeps one reasonably busy until the age of 75 – good health permitting.

The Lord Lieutenant is the sovereign's personal representative in the county.

Henry VIII first appointed Lord Lieutenants for the counties of England in the year 1536, at the time of the Pilgrimage of Grace. They were empowered 'to enquire of treason, misprision of treason, insurrection and riot, with authority to levy men and lead them against the king's enemies'. They thus took over military duties which had previously been carried out by the county sheriffs. From time to time the County Levy was called on in civil commotion, later this became the Fencibles, Volunteers, Militia, Royal Defence Corps and Home Guard, called out in periods of danger from abroad like the Armada in 1588, the threatened invasion by Napoleon in 1803 to 1805, and the two recent World Wars.

I am the 21st Lord Lieutenant of County Durham since 1536, although history does not record a holder of the office between 1580 and 1638 or between 1648 and 1660.

My predecessors have included three Bishops, no fewer than five members of the Vane family of Raby Castle, and three Marquesses of Londonderry whose County Durham seat was at Wynyard.

The Lord Lieutenant is no longer responsible for calling out any armed forces and indeed has not had that responsibility since the 19th century. However, a relic of that era is that he still requires

1990, PDN, the family, and Daisy.

the sovereign's permission to be out of the county for more than three weeks, in case a major crisis blows up in his county.

Our prime duties are to represent the sovereign within the county and specifically to look after visits by members of the Royal Family. Many of us hold the office of 'Keeper of the Rolls' of magistrates for our county, and chair what is called The Lord Chancellor's Advisory Committee which makes recommendations on the appointment and disciplinary of magistrates. A legacy of the old days is that we are actively involved with the 'Reserve Forces and Cadets Association' (RFCA) and if male, have a military style uniform worn on formal occasions. In general, we are expected to know what is going on in our county and set an example as good citizens, keeping clear of local politics.

Each Lord Lieutenant can appoint a number of deputies who then can use the letters 'DL' after their name. The numbers permitted depend on the population of the county and in Durham's case it is fifty. I try to select men and women who have made a significant contribution to the life of the county and to voluntary or local government organizations within its boundaries.

CHAPTER 8

Vaux in the Eighties

THE ELECTION OF Margaret Thatcher in 1979 completely changed the rules of the commercial and social game. Sir John Methven, probably the greatest Director General of the CBI, foresaw this at the time, when he forecast the eighties as an entirely new and very exciting era in which to be doing business.

Days of low productivity and slack management were over and we were entering a new world, tough, but far more rewarding for those who could adapt. Businessmen were to be free to run their businesses successfully or otherwise, but if not successful, then they would not be protected from market forces, even if this meant bankruptcy, redundancy or takeover.

Vaux's earnings per share only just managed to keep pace with inflation in the 1970s, increasing by 378% against inflation through that decade of 366%. In this it did better than most, but the story in the eighties was very different, earnings increased by 246% against inflation of 88%, so nearly 2.8 times the rate of inflation. Dividends actually went up over 3½ times that rate, making up for a shortfall of around 45% in the previous decade.

The strategy set in the 1970s remained successful right through the next decade, although it had its ups and downs. The decade started with a severe recession as inflation began to be brought under control, but then began a period of fast expansion right through until recession began to bite again in 1990.

I had some excellent help over the 1980s from non executive directors, particularly Tony Pearson, a North East industrialist with a full understanding of the problems and opportunities in the region, and Peter Vaux a member of the founding family. While the Vaux family stake was relatively small and widely dispersed, it still totalled around 7% in 1980. It was most helpful

Vaux employees, 1980.

to have his support. In 1985 Charles Tidbury, former Chairman of Whitbread, had joined our Board. During the five years he was with us he was a stimulating colleague. He made a major contribution to the Group at a time when we were to come under a lot of speculative pressure.

During my thirty-four years with the company, I was well served by three PAs. My first was Miss Blakey. In the sixties life was much more formal and I think Miss Blakey would have been horrified to be called by her Christian name of Marion. When she retired in the late 1970s she was succeeded by Pru Gillbanks, a very efficient doctor's daughter. She needed extra help as my duties expanded in the mid eighties and Marjorie Ford joined as a secretary. When Pru accepted a management position with the National Farmers Union, Marjorie became my PA. She was assisted by Patsy Smith until 1997 when the Development Corporation ceased. Marjorie came with me when I left but needed full-time work, which after two years I no longer had for her.

I usually drove myself, particularly from home the nineteen miles to my office, but I had two drivers in my time with the Company. The first was Reg Southall, who was the old fashioned sort. He retired in the early eighties, and then I had John White, who became and remains a friend and confidant. John's hobby used to be driving horses, but when he became my driver, he took up training dogs and shooting. His dogs are well trained and on the occasions John has come with me to load out shooting, I bask in the reflected glory of his dogs!

Much of the success of Vaux was due to its people. There were to be several thousands of these as the Group expanded. In the breweries however, numbers tended to decline. Productivity and efficiency improvements meant that in common with so much of industry there was less need for manufacturing jobs, but this was more than compensated, in Vaux's case, by increases in demand for service jobs. We tried hard to avoid compulsory redundancy and the numbers of these during my time with the company, apart from when we sold our Scottish brewing interests, could be counted in tens rather than hundreds.

I and my colleagues on the board tried to make everyone working for companies within the Vaux Group feel a pride in what the group and their company was doing. We were at the forefront of profit share schemes. Ours started in 1978 and over the next 20 years over 8 million shares, representing about 6% of the final share capital, were issued to employees under this scheme. When the Save As You Earn (SAYE) scheme was introduced, we took full advantage of such an opportunity and assuming that those SAYE options outstanding at the time of the Whitbread offer were taken up, over 3 million shares were issued under this scheme. While the majority of those who acquired profit and SAYE shares quickly sold them on, there were some who did not. The average employee in the schemes from the early days could have accumulated over £30,000 worth by 1999.

Linking people below senior management who work in a company to its long term performance is no longer fashionable, except in a few enlightened groups like Tesco. The seventies and eighties up until the time of the miners' strike in 1984 were an era of highly volatile labour relations. This was particularly so in the brewing industry. Our policies meant Vaux largely avoided such problems. We picked up a lot of trade in consequence and probably had the best labour relations in our industry. This was not of course only due to share schemes. We had works and retail councils, briefing groups and at one time quality circles, although the latter did not take off for us. Possibly unique was the Vaux 'Empire Show' when up to three times a year presentations were given in the local theatre to all those within reach of Sunderland on how the company was doing. These were in the eighties led by myself, with supporting presentations from other directors. A similar event was held in Sheffield.

We adopted as far as we could a similar approach to these presentations as in our annual 'Vaux Open Day' presentations to the City. Indeed in order to counter any suspicion that what we told the City did not fit in with what we told our people, we in later years, had members of our works councils alongside senior and middle management attending our open day rehearsal. While some of what we were planning to tell the City, particularly about the complications of finance, might have been a little over the heads of some brewery operatives, I tried to make light of this by talking about 'City Slickers', a term they could all understand!

In the seventies while we had a final salary pension scheme for staff, we had only a sub-standard money purchase scheme for brewery operatives. I changed this to one final salary scheme, although in the late eighties we did introduce a supplementary scheme for senior staff to bring down their retirement age to 60. It was becoming fashionable to consider senior management too old beyond 60. The fashion seems now to be rapidly changing as it has become apparent just how expensive this is.

There were several years during the seventies and early eighties when we topped up our pension scheme from profits. This enabled the scheme to pay existing pensioners increases to match inflation beyond what it was contractually bound to pay.

Some of the people most important to the company's success were the several hundred tenants and managers of the individual pubs and hotels. Vaux always had a high reputation for pubs and its 'Swallow Hotels'. We tried to look after people in the pubs and hotels as they were at the sharp end of what we as a vertically integrated company were trying to achieve. We had close and cordial relations with our tenants through their own consultative committees. We also held up to ten annual 'chairman lunches' around the North for tenants together with hotel and pub managers, usually at the nearest Swallow Hotel.

I believe we attracted a higher degree of loyalty and commitment from our tenants, certainly than was prevalent in the larger companies or is now the norm for many 'pubcos'. These have high property rents on top of even higher rake-offs from the supply of those products they allow their tenants to stock. It is always surprising to me that the 'pubcos' as property owners can still get away with these two streams of income. It is a major factor in keeping up the price of beer.

Another group of people we paid a lot of attention to were our personal shareholders. There were some 8000 outside private individuals with shares in Vaux plus some 2000 employees. Our annual general meetings were social affairs attended at times by over 600 individual shareholders. At none of the 22 AGMs I chaired did we ever have any serious dissension and hardly any awkward questions. The meetings were followed by a sumptuous and liquid buffet. Possibly anticipation of this inhibited questioning! However I always tried to give the meeting a concise but comprehensive briefing of what was going on, covering the main issues which I planned to discuss at our 'open day' a few days later. Following a tip from Ewart Boddington, who had successfully fought off a bid for his company from Allied Breweries, I started to send a personal 'topped and tailed' letter of welcome to every new outside private shareholder whose name appeared on our register.

I was never myself a 'people person', being of a reserved disposition, but Richard Pettit, who in the early eighties ran the brewing and pub side, naturally related to people, while his successor, my brother Frank, has a very friendly manner and an outstanding memory for names and details about people he has met at all levels. Peter Catesby had a rather different style being more authoritarian but this was appropriate for a multi site operation.

A major event for the company coinciding with the start of the Thatcher era was the sale of our main Scottish brewing operation and pubs to Allied Breweries in January 1980. Our Scottish end at that time represented over 20% of our assets, but less than 10% of our trading profits. We had tried many initiatives to correct our Scottish problem. While some, such as the launch of Norseman in 1973, had enjoyed short-term success, the fundamental problem was that we were competing against a virtual duopoly of Scottish Brewers and the Bass subsidiary Tennants. No one else enjoyed longer-term success in this situation. Allied Breweries hoped that the acquisition of our interests merged with their own would enable them to compete more effectively, but this did not happen.

We obtained a good price for the sale but our problem then was 'What do we do with the cash?' In today's climate the answer would almost certainly have been to return it to shareholders, but when we investigated this at the time, it would have triggered major problems, including possible redemption of low coupon debentures. In any case share buybacks and special dividends were virtually unknown. We did make generous provision for those who lost their jobs as a result of the sale and closure. In a climate where labour attitudes had not really begun to change from those of the seventies, these must have been perceived as fair by the parties involved, as there was no industrial trouble.

The Thatcher era had led initially to a severe recession as the excesses of socialism had to be squeezed out. Our then much smaller hotel division saw its profits fall nearly 30% over 1979-1981. Rationalization of our brewing and pubs interest more than countered this but it did make us cautious until signs of a strong recovery emerged in 1982, with Swallow Hotels more than making up its earlier shortfall.

We reinforced our beer and pub business with a move into off licences. We had always had a substantial wines and spirits business supplying our pubs and hotels and first owned off licences when in the early 1970s we bought from the Blayney family their four shops and two pubs in Newcastle. Off licences were an opportunity which fitted into our strategy of extending into related businesses. By the end of the 1970s we had 50 outlets. In 1981 I put our off licences into a separate division under Anthony Wood.

By 1982 Swallow's profits had recovered and as the 1980s expansion gathered pace we became bolder about hotel building and acquisitions. Our first substantial new build since the early seventies had been a 123-bedroom hotel (subsequently expanded) just by exit 28 off the M1 motorway. This was opened in 1981 but it was in March 1982 that we made one of our most significant moves. This was the acquisition of the 417-room London International Hotel on the Cromwell Road. The Hotel had been put up for sale by Sir Maxwell Joseph's Grand Metropolitan Hotels as he was refocusing his group towards the five star market with his acquisition of Intercontinental Hotels. Sir Maxwell had in the sixties and seventies been one of the most feared take-over kings of his day. His successful battles for Trumans and Watneys Breweries made his Grand Metropolitan Group one of the most aggressive groups of the era. It had weathered a severe economic storm in 1974 when it nearly went under, but came through strongly thereafter.

We had of course had earlier dealings in 1972 with Sir Maxwell, when buying out his minority interest in Wards. He was a formidable negotiator, who liked to do major deals personally. It was thus that I found myself opposite him seeking to buy this London Hotel. We agreed an early stage on a handshake, what I thought was a reasonable price, but when it came to the detail, he sought to win every point. However, it remained a good deal and eventually I told him yes, I would take it on his terms. At this his response was, 'I wish you had not said that, you see I have had a much higher offer.'

He could legally have walked away at any stage during negotiations on the detail, but he was of the older school, of 'my word is my bond'. It was an object lesson to me and one which I always tried to follow thereafter. During the Vaux problems of 1999 I related this story widely, but was told that such behaviour was completely out of date!

While Swallow drove much of the growth during the 1980s, it also absorbed the lion's share of the investment, some £120 million as opposed to £70 million in the Breweries. Swallow's trading profits grew by some 8½ times, as against around 3 times for the rest of the business.

Peter Catesby was in charge of Swallow from 1973 until taking over as Chief Executive of the Group for the few months, in 1999, covering destruction of the breweries and the sale of the rump of the company. He was an able hotelier. Trained on the old Trust House model, he had come to Vaux shortly after the Forte takeover of that company. Most of the credit for the success of Swallow is due to him, although when times were tough as in 1979-81, and again in 1990-93 he needed a lot of help and support, particularly during the latter recession against the senior non-executive director, Stephen Gibbs, who looked for his scalp.

He was supported by a good team. Standing out were Ermes Oretti the Swallow director responsible for most of the new builds and major hotel developments and Roger Carrigan whose initiative it was to set up the 'North East Businessman of the Year' promotion, together with the *Journal* newspaper. This was probably the most successful promotional initiative the Group ever undertook. It was largely self funding in that places for the awards dinner were always sold out. It attracted over the years a very distinguished list of principal guests including the Duke of Edinburgh and three Prime Ministers, Margaret Thatcher, John Major and Tony Blair, who was the last principal guest at a dinner just after the Group had been sold out to Whitbread. I was not invited to this!

In general I was able to delegate most of the Swallow operations to Peter, only sometimes having to restrain his enthusiasm for certain acquisitions which I considered of dubious merit. There was however one major hotel acquisition we both would very much have liked to have made, which got away. In 1983 I was approached by the Managing Director of de Vere Hotels, with a view to Vaux acquiring their substantial portfolio of some 14 hotels. I made the mistake of using Morgan Grenfell to advise on this negotiation. We had recently appointed them, under pressure from the City as our joint corporate finance advisors. Noble Grossart were our other advisor who had done an excellent job in previous negotiations but were based in Edinburgh, and have never been part of the City 'mafia'. A deal was agreed in 1984 but foundered on the insistence of the 82 year old major shareholder to be paid in cash up front. Morgans said they could not raise the £40 million necessary for this. I felt I had to respect their judgement. At the time I was under a certain strain personally as Sarah had been diagnosed with breast cancer. However we certainly should have been able to raise the money and would have, I believe, if we had used Noble Grossart. A month or so after our deal with de Vere collapsed, Greenalls acquired them. They did not have a very auspicious start as it was in one of their newly acquired hotels, The Grand at Brighton, that the IRA bomb went off at the Conservative 1984 conference. I was quite relieved at the time that this was not my problem!

We were to grow increasingly unhappy with Morgans. They had been advisors to Bells, and when Guinness made their bid, Raymond Miguel the Bells Chairman was shocked to find it was Morgans who had a large amount of insider information about his company who were acting for Guinness. We were in a very similar position to Bells, and were extremely concerned that Morgans might act for a predator. We changed our advisors to Lazards. Fortunately after the Guinness scandal, Morgans' credibility was largely destroyed.

I was more directly concerned with the brewing and pubs side both within the company, and within the industry. After the sale of Lorimers, almost all our pubs were in the North of England. Two of the strands of the strategy which I had set the Group in the seventies, were to increase market share, within the main trading area, the North East, and to develop in adjacent areas. During the eighties we did achieve both these objectives, but it was tougher going against strong competition from a reinvigorated Scottish and Newcastle under Alick Rankin's leadership.

In the early eighties Richard Pettit looked after the Sunderland Breweries and pubs, it was he who suggested that we brought into the company my youngest brother Frank Nicholson, who previous to joining Vaux was a Chartered Surveyor in London. Frank joined in 1982 to look after our pubs, when I had moved Anthony Wood to develop our wine and spirit wholesale and retail operations, which I saw as a growth opportunity.

In 1984 personal problems prompted Richard to resign and Frank took his place, although he didn't join the board until 1987. Both he and Richard before him were strong on industrial relations, and dealing with people. They handled the often tricky Sunderland annual wage negotiations. Michael Wright looked after Wards brewery and Darleys brewery which we had acquired in 1979. In head office we had Peter Heyward, a kind of father figure, until his retirement in 1987.

I had a much more 'hands on' part in the development of the

breweries and pubs with Richard then Frank, Michael Wright and Peter Heyward reporting directly to me. It was not always successful, I was responsible for one near disastrous investment in a loan to a chain of leased amusement bars called Dingwalls. This went bankrupt, leaving us with onerous leases as the only security for the £1 million or so we had lent them. I had been taken in, if not conned, by the proprietor, a prominent member of the Young Presidents Organization. The trading potential had looked interesting but neither he nor ourselves knew how to run what were actually night clubs. It caused me many sleepless nights, although eventually an improvement in the overall market enabled us to dispose of the leases to operators who understood the business without too big a loss.

The Labour era had made me feel that it was sensible not to have all eggs in the UK basket. We had gone into Belgium with the acquisition of Liefmans in 1974, designed to give us a foothold in the European Economic Community as it was then known. After the sale of Lorimers, an opportunity arose through a friend in the Australian corporate finance world, for a joint venture running pubs in the Melbourne area. We entered into this.

While Australia was a long way to go it always appeared to have attractive opportunities. Our partner in Australia, a pub group owned by the Carlyon family, seemed well placed with several outlets already in the state of Victoria. The partnership never quite realized its potential, partly because the chief executive of our partner company had another partnership in which he was rather more interested, owning race horses with Robert Sangster!

Since the sixties when I attended a Harvard marketing course I had thought that if the opportunity arose we should look to invest in the States. Thanks to Dick Carlsberg and his introduction to the Young Presidents I became even more determined to try and find a US investment. Thus when Fritz Maytag, the owner of the Anchor Steam Brewery in San Francisco and the godfather of the American boutique brewing world, gave me an introduction to the Fred Koch Brewery in upstate New York, I thought it looked a good bet.

We bought Kochs for $2m in1981. I sent Stuart Wilson, who had been second brewer in Sunderland, over to run it. We believed the time was ripe for developing 'niche' brewers in the States where premium beers were becoming popular. Stuart worked manfully to establish this but we were ahead of our time. Kochs struggled to achieve near break-even in 1983 and when further losses were made in1984 we decided to sell. The losses were mitigated because I had bought it with an exchange rate of nearly two dollars to the pound and sold it when the exchange rate was near one dollar to the pound. Stuart remained in the States and left our employ for a time. We were however very pleased to welcome him back a year later to become Head Brewer in Sunderland and subsequently Operations Director in overall charge of the groups production and distribution. He was a leading member of the team which tried to save the breweries in 1999.

Having overseas operations was a fun challenge, but I was not prepared to bet the shop. This cautious approach meant that, in spite of consuming an inordinate amount of travel time and personal energy, the Vaux overseas ventures never really worked, so by 1986 we had exited from all of them. They did not overall add value for our shareholders but they were not a disaster. In the meantime I and a number of my colleagues had had our eyes opened to different worlds.

There were a number of amusing incidents involved with our overseas ventures. During one visit I attended the US Brewers convention in San Diego. The famous August Busch IV was in the chair. His family firm Anheuser Busch was and remains the largest and most successful brewer anywhere.

He, however, was not the typical 'hail fellow well met' American Chief Executive. At the conference he was surrounded by his minions, and certainly in that company the age of deference was far from dead. They did not exactly tug their forelocks when addressing him, but it was always 'Yes Mr Busch' or 'No Mr Busch' as required to agree with him.

One venture which was profitable for Vaux Shareholders was our involvement in Television. In the late seventies the North East

▲ Paul Nicholson – the driving force behind the consortium.

NORSEMAN – aiming to rid the North of its 'Andy Capp' image

● ON DECEMBER 23 the Independent Broadcasting Authority will announce the decision which will seal the future of television broadcasting in the North East. Three groups are in the running for the franchise – present holders Tyne Tees, TV North, whose case we examined recently, and Norseman Television, whose inspiration and driving force is Paul Nicholson, Chairman of Vaux Breweries. This month we talk to Nicholson, who outlines Norseman's case.

1980, PDN During the Norseman Bid for Tyne Tees Television franchise (reproduced courtesy of The Journal*).*

TV monopoly was owned by Trident Television who also owned Yorkshire. Trident had been set up in the sixties, the original aim was that the third prong of the 'Trident' should have been Anglia TV, but they never managed to achieve this. All the TV franchises had been due to be put out to tender in 1978, but the Independent Television Corporation (ITC), the quango who regulated TV in those days, had extended these franchises until 1981. I was asked to join a group called Northumbria Television to try and overturn the ITC decision so that we could bid. While this approach did not get far, a number of us who had been involved decided we should go for the North East Franchise when it was put out to tender. The nucleus of our group, which we called 'Norseman', besides myself, were Richard Storey, Chairman of Portsmouth and Sunderland Newspapers, Dennis Stevenson who had recently completed a spell as Chairman of Peterlee and Newton Aycliffe new towns and Joe Mills of the Transport and General Workers Union. We recruited Robin Gill a former Managing Director of Border Television as our main consultant.

Applicants had to prepare detailed plans and costings of what they would provide. Basically we had to convince the ITC that we would offer the best service for the region. The incumbent holder of the Northeast franchise, Tyne Tees Television, having been put on alert by the Northumbria attempt, had in the meantime considerably improved their service. However we gathered an impressive team to our consortium including Denise Robertson the authoress, Fred Holliday, Vice Chancellor of Durham University and Diana Eccles now Baroness Eccles of Moulton. Over the summer we held public meetings throughout the region to explain why we considered that we were better and to enlist support. This culminated in a grand meeting in Newcastle convened by the ITC, whose board were present. There we, as well as another challenger and the incumbent each had 10 minutes to present our case before an audience selected by the ITC from a wide range of interests within the region. We had already had a formal meeting with the commission. I was somewhat put out when I kept strictly within my allocated time, being on first, while the others were way over their time, and were not pulled up.

The time for announcing the decision was fixed between Christmas and New Year, and the ITC stated that they required senior representatives of each bidding party to be present at their headquarters in London at this highly inconvenient time. I was very reluctant to go, as a fairly strong leak had emerged that the incumbent was going to be granted the franchise. On arrival at the ITC headquarters, I was ushered into a small room, where an ITC official with a grim face, told me in a funereal voice that he was afraid we had not been successful. I think he was expecting me to burst into tears at the news, and was somewhat put out when I thanked him and left to go straight back to resume my Christmas break.

While we had lost the battle it subsequently emerged as far as I was concerned that I had actually won the war. Trident was compulsorily broken up and independence was restored to a substantial North East company with Vaux able to take a 20% stake at a cost of £1 million. As a condition of Vaux taking a stake, I was able to insist that I and one other from our consortium should join the board. The existing Tyne Tees directors jibbed at the idea of having Richard Storey because of what they perceived as his competing newspaper interest. He was Chairman of Portsmouth and Sunderland Newspapers. Dennis Stevenson was mutually agreed as the most suitable. For some years in the early eighties, having an independent company holding the regional monopoly was of great benefit, particularly as its Chairman Sir Ralph Carr-Ellison did so much for the region. However the world moved on, the monopoly was broken with the advent of Channel 4 and a remerger with Yorkshire occurred in 1990 with the Vaux stake then worth £5 million being sold. I was invited however to remain a director of the merged company. After the merger there were considerable problems in Yorkshire, Ward Thomas who had been the original Chairman of Trident but had come over to Tyne Tees in 1981 was able to step in as a new Chairman of the Group. He brought in as Chief Executive Bruce Gyngall previously of TVAM.

Yorkshire then flourished until it itself was taken over in an uncontested bid by Granada in 1997 whereupon I and the rest of the Yorkshire Tyne Tees board bowed out.

The ventures overseas and into television might have been deviations from our main strategy. They did the group no harm overall and indeed taking the decade as a whole did add value.

So far as our main strategy was concerned, hotels and beer were doing well and our off-licences chain was building up. One of our major off licence moves was the acquisition from Camerons Brewery, by then owned by the Barclay twins, David and Frederick, of their chain. We had put in an offer for this, but heard nothing until I was rung up while at Kochs in America at around 4 a.m. Eastern American time. I was told my offer was an insult, to which I replied somewhat blearily, that I was not going to increase it. A few hours later I received another call saying it was ours! I am a considerable admirer of what the twins have achieved. They are at least decisive!

The business was a successful extension over this period and while in relation to the other main businesses of brewing and of hotels, it was relatively small, accounting at its peak for around 5% of Group trading profits, nevertheless it was an important part of our success story and realized a healthy capital return when sold on in 1991.

The main threat to the company in the eighties was of a bid. None ever materialized. A lot of money may have been made by less desirable elements in the finance world, ramping the shares which were once described as having been 'punted more often than the ball at Twickenham'. I may have deterred bids by taking an extremely aggressive approach in public statements, open days etc, as well as behind the scenes, making clear that Vaux was not for sale, and any bidder would have to pay dearly. Nevertheless, much of my time and mental energy, particularly in the latter half of the decade was devoted to resisting potential bids.

I observed closely other bids in the sector. Guinness under 'Deadly' Ernest Saunders set the scene first with the bid for Bells, where a vicious and unfair advertising campaign; 'Bells has lost its way' was waged against its target. The 'takeover panel' following their usual practice only banned such a tactic after the damage had been done. The subsequent intervention by Guinness as a 'White Knight' for Distillers in their battle with Argyle led as is well known to Saunders and two others being 'Guests of Her Majesty' although I am far from certain that their crime of agreeing to compensate those who supported their share price was that heinous. There was politics involved with Ministers facing an election and pandering to a media baying for blood.

Vaux only intervened twice in other battles. The first time was by submitting a formal objection to the Office of Fair Trading against an agreed takeover of Cameron Brewery of Hartlepool by Scottish and Newcastle (S and N). S and N were already the largest brewer in the North East by a substantial margin and if they had been allowed to take over Camerons who were number three, this would have made life much harder for Vaux. The bid was referred to the Monopolies Commission and then withdrawn.

The other time was during S and N's first bid for Matthew Browne of Blackburn when we bought shares in Matthew Browne to help thwart S and N's attack. Unfortunately for Matthew Browne, they were so weakened by the cost of fighting off that bid that when a year or so later S and N came back, they failed to see them off a second time and succumbed. However this was at a substantially higher price than the first bid, so Vaux made a decent profit.

I met the Australian aggressor John Elliot for the first time in the famous Berkeley Square night club 'Annabel's'. He had launched a bid for Allied Lyons and was in the middle of that battle at the time. I had been attending a dinner of 'the great and the good' of the brewing industry which included Allied's Chairman, Sir Derrick Holden Browne. After dinner Alick Rankin and I took our respective wives on to Annabel's. There we found John Elliot and a young lady sitting in a corner, we recognized him from his press photos. We bearded him, introducing ourselves and our wives. He was somewhat embarrassed as he introduced the girl with him as his 'corporate advisor' from 'Citicorp'. We told him that he would not be successful in his bid for Allied to which his reply was 'Want a bet?!'. Alick and I said 'OK £10' to which his contemptuous retort was – 'I meant a proper bet!'. I am not a betting man but Alick and I were shamed into increasing our bets to £100. When his bid for Allied lapsed, I was determined to be paid. I sought payment through Mike Hamson, a mutual friend living in Australia, and also Michael Cotterill of Courage Breweries which Elliot had bought from Hanson after his Allied bid failed. Eventually I received a cheque from John to which he had generously added some £10 interest for late payment!

After he bought Courage he became involved in a battle royal with Alick Rankin, when he tried to take over Scottish and Newcastle. Alick outsmarted him and he retired hurt to Australia, where he subsequently faced prosecution for breaches of Australian company law, but was eventually acquitted. By this time he had left the brewing industry.

In January 1985 the *Sunday Telegraph* had listed Vaux among an undistinguished group of companies as likely to be taken over. This excited one of our Corporate Finance advisors Morgan Grenfell who possibly anticipated some juicy fees. While we never actually had a bid, we knew of at least two potential predators stalking us. We kept a very close eye on our share register, serving notices under section 212 of the Companies Act on nominee holdings to try and identify any build-ups. We noticed in late '86 holdings being built up in the name of two or three Banks which 212 notices revealed as having been bought by Rowe and Pitman. Notices served on them produced the reply that these holdings were held beneficially for Rothschilds. Believing the word 'beneficial', we did not pursue the matter. However, in January 1987 Judy Bevan, a respected *Sunday Times* reporter, got wind of a scoop that Wolverhampton and Dudley had acquired a 4.9% stake. The Rothschild shares turned out not to have been beneficial for them, but in fact held for Wolverhampton.

I asked David Thompson managing director of Wolverhampton Brewery and his uncle David Miller, who was shortly to take over as Chairman, to come and see me. They arrived on a Sunday afternoon, where with my brother Frank as a witness, I sat them down in my living room and expressed to them my fury at the deception and sent them packing with fleas in their ears. By this time the story had broken, and to regularize the situation, Wolverhampton had gone over 5% which under the Companies Act triggered them having to go public about their holding. I think David Miller was particularly embarrassed by what I had told them. He told me several years later how he had expressed his views to all concerned.

The law states that once 5% has been acquired, a further declaration has to be made for every 1%, acquired, however we decided to serve daily 212 notices on Wolverhampton to harass them, until they agreed they would not acquire further shares without pre-notifying us.

We sought an investigation into the misleading responses to 212 notices through the DTI but in its usual inimitable fashion the City closed ranks. Rowe and Pitman were after all the royal stockbrokers, and no wrongdoing could be proved. However, Wolverhampton realizing what a hornets' nest they had stirred up, then quietly, and in full co-operation with us, placed their holding through our broker Cazenove a few months later in May 1987.

There were a number of other excitements including a message delivered to me at our 1988 AGM 'Could I ring Cyril Stein Chairman of Ladbrokes'. That company had been frequently speculated about as a bidder for us. In some trepidation I called him back with other board members listening, but the call turned out to be in relation to negotiations on care homes and not sinister in any way.

More serious however, was the discovery of a holding by the New Zealand speculator Ron Brierley of 2%. This was sold to Queens Moat who gradually built up a holding of near 10% by 1990. I had discussions with the Queens Moat Chairman, John Bairstow, in which I made clear to him that I saw no synergies between our two companies.

In 1990 Queens Moat had used their hyped and inflated share price to make a successful contested and all share take over of

THE GUARDIAN 19TH FEBRUARY 1987

In defence of a brewer at bay

Peter Hetherington reports on Vaux's fight to preserve jobs in Sunderland by staying independent

Delivering the old way, but Paul Nicholson (right) is looking to the future

THE BREWERY, standing high above the River Wear in the centre of Sunderland, is more than just a symbol of a favourite North-east pastime. With the shipyards still declining, subsidiary engineering factories flattened, and — most disturbing of all — the newer electronics plants long since gone, the Vaux Group is the biggest private employer in the town.

More significantly, with a current market capitalisation of £230 million, a workforce nationally of 5,000 — 3,300 in the North-east and 1,400 in Sunderland. — it is the second largest private company in the region as well as a mainstay of the economy in a town where one in five is jobless.

Yet for over 20 years Vaux, managed by the same family since it was founded in 1806, has been the subject of periodical takeover speculation. Earlier this month the rumours started again. A Midlands brewer, Wolverhampton and Dudley, had acquired a 5 per cent stake in the company. The share price rose to 580p.

The local radio reported that a takeover was imminent. Managers shuddered. Mr Paul Nicholson, the chairman, was philosophical. He has been through it all before. " This is at least the fourth time in my memory — first 1963, when the fever was just as high as it is today. There was a run in 1968, another very high level (of share buying) in '72-'73, more in '77 then it died away until '84."

In his modest Sunderland office beside the brewery, with a blue spiral book at hand — " City code on takeovers and mergers and rules governing substantial acquisition of shares " — Mr Nicholson explains the continual dilemma : " We have on and off been speculated about because there is no substantial controlling shareholding (Vaux went public in 1926) so obviously it's possible to take us over compared with cer-

uous speculation and it's not helpful on the shop floor — a nuisance to put it mildly. If it goes on I'm sure with some companies it becomes a sort of self-fulfilling prophecy. Everyone expects it to happen and it's very difficult to manage the company and to make it go forward. I'm not saying we've reached that stage but I can foresee the danger."

So is he anxious ? No, he says, just concerned. Of course, any takeover could make him a " very rich man," but the well-being of a successful and expanding company — which is actually increasing jobs — is paramount. " But we can't face short-termism . . . people

Guardian *article, 1987.*

Norfolk Capital Hotels. We had grave suspicions as to the viability of Queens Moat, and I think Bairstow may have realized that a move against us would have released these suspicions on the market, bringing forward that company's subsequent collapse.

Those city institutions who took Queens Moat shares for their Norfolk Holdings lost a packet. I could not resist chiding them with how lucky they were never to have had such a temptation put in their way for Vaux. Anyhow, the Queens Moat holding was disposed of during 1991 and while some of this was picked up by Whitbread investments, there were no other threatening stakes built up.

I have always held a strong belief that while there is obviously a price for everything, there are wider issues than short-term shareholder value. I do not disagree with the view that shareholder value is a prime concern of management, but it is, at the end of the day, only a scorecard. A Company needs a vision, and needs to believe in what it is doing. It needs standards of ethics and conduct towards its customers, employees, and the community. I have never been in the business of dealing in businesses although in pursuing the company's objectives I bought businesses and particularly closed, or sold businesses where they no longer fitted in.

CHAPTER 9

Vaux – The Final Years

A CHAIRMAN OF A substantial PLC has to have at least some profile in the financial press even if his company is not in the FTSE 100. Vaux was for most of my time around the middle of the next layer the FTSE 250. In a speech to Scottish Financial enterprise in 1989 I quoted two headlines, one from the *Daily Mail* 'Vaux Chairman denies bid as shares soar', and the other from the *Guardian* 'Vaux hits at bid rumours'. The difference being they were 25 years apart. Except for a period between 1977-1984 when it was thought brewery takeovers would not be allowed, I could probably find in my scrap book a similar quote from a national newspaper covering almost every year I worked for the company.

I can never claim to have had an easy relationship with the financial press and particularly with the 'City' in its widest context covering the plethora of brokers, institutions, corporate financiers and just plain spivs, who inhabit the square mile or its periphery. Managers of joint stock companies may have, as my company did, many thousands of individual shareholders and we welcomed these, but most companies would find that their ten to twenty largest shareholders effectively controlled the company with over half the votes. This situation arose because of high taxation on individuals and special tax treatment for pension funds, unit trusts, and until recently life insurance.

We have over the past few decades reached a situation where probably less than 100 institutions own the majority of the shares in all plcs except founder or family dominated companies. This is a fact of life and not necessarily bad in itself. However as so few of them are now mutuals, they themselves are owned in a similar way to the companies they invest in, having shareholders of their own. Their worship at the altar of 'shareholder value' leads all too often to short termist pressures on the companies they invest in.

Ironically in a number of cases it is not making money per se that drives them, so much as outperforming benchmarks. Huge bonuses are paid to executives even in a downturn, if they have lost marginally less money than competitors, but few institutions dare defy the consensus. They gain little credit if they get it right and severe brickbats and loss of business when in the short term they get it wrong. Philips and Drew Fund Managers were three years ago suffering a near melt down of lost customers because they did not back the 'New Economy bubble'. In this region they had two local authority pensions funds but lost one. Two years later after the bubble had burst they were top of the pops, but I suspect few of those who deserted them rushed to return.

I took a high profile in the press and before every audience I could find in criticizing the general culture of bids, making it clear that I was not against bids for failing companies, but it was nonsense to maintain that all bids were for such companies. The evidence was that in the majority of cases long term value was not added. Look at a five year view of Granada. Only those who cashed in have made much from their hotels takeover, where the Granada management singularly failed to run hotels as well as the Fortes.

I have found City ethics distinctly dubious. As I said earlier, Vaux shares have been described as having been punted more often than the ball at Twickenham. While we could never find where the stories came from, they were obviously inspired in the City. Particularly distasteful is the holier than thou attitude adopted by certain institutions who jump on the corporate governance bandwagon, except where it concerns executive remuneration. Executive pay was not a particular issue until the invention of 'Remuneration Committees'. Now in both Britain and America executive compensation is reaching ever more obscene levels and what are the institutions doing about it – nothing! Many are themselves the worst offenders. The remuneration packages for directors of that self appointed 'cheerleader' of corporate governances Hermes are typical of such hypocrisy.

I must however accept that continued takeover speculation about Vaux kept us on our toes, but it also diverted an enormous amount of time and nervous energy to shoring up our defences rather than developing the business.

Possibly my highest profile stance in public was in a Bank of England Debate held in March 1989 in the Bank on the motion, '*this House believes that contested bids tend to be bad for Industry*.' I was approached some months before by Jonathan Charkham a director of the Bank of England and invited to propose the motion, in a debate sponsored by an organization called the Treasurers Society. Why me I wondered? But I was flattered to be asked, and as it was a subject on which I felt strongly, I accepted. He was obviously mightily relieved to have found someone foolhardy enough to put such a motion in the heart of the 'City'. It became obvious that there were much bigger Captains of Industry who had declined to put their heads above the parapet, particularly when they were told that the motion was to be opposed by Sir James Goldsmith.

Anyhow the day for the debate dawned, the venue was in the basement of the bank, which had been set up like a public school debating society chamber, with myself and Sir John Harvey Jones, my seconder, (he had declined to propose because he was no longer Chairman of a plc), on one side, and Sir James Goldsmith with his seconder Martin Taylor (not the former Barclays Bank Chief Executive, but the then Vice Chairman of Hanson) on the other. What I had not sufficiently appreciated was that the majority of the audience were from City institutions who made their living from contested bids. In front of such an audience, few industrialists who were there would want to be seen supporting such a motion!

My case had a number of strands. I pointed out that hostile takeover bids were a relatively recent innovation of the fifties and that they were at that time a phenomenon almost exclusively of Anglo Saxon economies. While agreeing that not all contested takeovers were bad, there was a lot of evidence that most did not achieve the objectives of the aggressor and often the only longer term beneficiaries were those investors in the target company who sold out for cash. I commented that while management had a prime duty to shareholders, they also had responsibilities to customers and to loyal employees, but the biggest responsibility was to the public interest. Moves which brought the ethos of capitalism into disrepute were in the long term damaging.

The debate was held when the notorious Guinness affair was fresh in public minds and I said I believed that standards of integrity had too often been compromised in takeover bids. Whereas the old ethics of the city had been 'my word is my bond'. Now bending the rules was considered clever, as long as the 11th commandment 'thou shalt not get caught' was not broken. I commented that sanctions from the Takeover Panel and the Department of Trade, who were at the time the main regulators, lacked teeth.

I told the audience that coming as I did from the North, I had seen what had happened to employment and the regional economy when indigenous firms were taken over by outsiders. I pointed out that while the North was a peripheral region of England, the whole of Britain might itself suffer the same fate tacked on as we were to the North West corner of Europe.

I also argued that we businessmen were monopolists at heart. Winning the competitive battle meant monopoly, and exploitation of the consumer and many takeovers, either aggressive or otherwise, were in effect short cuts to monopoly by eliminating competition.

In my conclusion I pointed out that some 50 to 100 institutions owned between them a majority voting stake in most PLCs, that these were a small un-elected clique resulting from an accident of our tax system which allowed special privileges for pensions and (at the time) life assurance. These institutions had a very narrow and short term interest which most of the time did not coincide with the public interest.

However as for the debate itself after the opening salvoes not one speaker from the floor spoke up on my side, while when the summing up came, Goldsmith was at his inspirational best. One could have thought contested takeovers were the salvation of the Universe! I am afraid my summing up was lame in comparison and the vote was overwhelmingly in his favour, although certain people sidled up to me later saying, we really agreed with what you said but we could not be seen to vote for you – A good commentary on City morality!

I had a nice letter from the Governor of the Bank of England, from which I quote:

> I thought that you battled splendidly against a very skilled antagonist and a degree of prejudice in the majority of the assembled company. It was not possible for the vote to show the extent to which even those who supported contested takeovers may have many of the anxieties and reservations which you expressed eloquently and which, to a great extent, I personally share with you...

and from the Governor of the Bank of Scotland:

> ...congratulations on your submission. If I may say so, it was excellent. In such a company where the ability to mount successful takeover bids is taken to be synonymous with virility, it was unlikely that managerial ability, which is what really matters, would get much sympathy. The extreme of this view was reached by Goldsmith in his summing up with his extraordinary and demonstrably untrue generalization that only badly managed companies were taken over. I hope the chauvinistic obsession with takeovers will gradually come to be seen to be as outmoded a method of achieving managerial change as blood letting and surgery without anaesthetics were in health care, but it will take time and persuasion. The trouble is, of course, that not all bids, not even all contested ones, are bad but there are too few of the people who were present whose experience would have enabled them to put such cases in perspective and to show that organic change works better, though less glamorously...

I represented Vaux in industry matters particularly the Brewers Society, where I sat on the Executive Committee for some 28 years. We met during most of that time each month. Brewing being part of the alcohol industry is high profile, as are pubs, where draconian licensing laws to control drinking during World War One were being slowly relaxed.

It was only during the eighties that the government ceased to be brewers and pub operators themselves, selling off their Carlisle and Invergordan operations which had been nationalized during the First World War, in an attempt to regulate drinking by munitions workers. Family legend has it, that at that time, the brewers were preparing to consent to the whole industry being nationalized, and it was only my grandfather who objected and stopped this happening.

Negotiating with Government over taxation, licensing and alcohol issues required a strong trade body. Unfortunately this gave a perception of the industry which was actually far from reality. To outsiders the impression was of a cosy, uncompetitive club and this was part of the reason why the industry was referred to the Monopolies Commission as a Complex Monopoly.

A serious tactical error was made when the major brewers decided that the case against the allegation of a complex monopoly should be put to the commission by an industry delegation sponsored by the Brewers Society with a leading QC arguing for us. It would have been much better if companies had put their cases individually.

The delegation was too high powered. It was led by Ian Prosser, then number two at Bass, and had as members senior representatives of all the major brewers of the time. They were Peter Jarvis of Whitbread, John McGrath then of Watneys, subsequently Chief Executive of Diageo, Mike Foster then of Courage, Richard Martin of Allied and Alick Rankin of Scottish.

I was the member of the delegation representing what was loosely defined as the 'regional brewers' made up of similar sized companies to ourselves such as Greenalls, Greene King and Marstons. Peter Robinson of Robinsons Brewery, Stockport, and Anthony Fuller represented the smaller companies.

Such a powerful delegation only reinforced the perception of the public and the commission that we were indeed a 'complex monopoly' whatever the arguments.

The commission sat appropriately in Carey Street. The case was heard by a panel of commissioners chaired by an academic, a Professor Smethurst, with panel members largely drawn from former 'apparatchiks' of major companies such as an ex-secretary of ICI. The most sensible and perceptive of the panel members was the trade unionist Lief Mills of the Inland Revenue Staff Federation, who from his questions at formal hearings, at least seemed to understand what he was talking about.

The whole atmosphere was unreal, certainly one, if not two of the commissioners seemed asleep during much of the proceedings. From where I sat, the only factor relieving some of the tedium was watching the comings and goings of the 'bouncing Czech' – Robert Maxwell's – helicopter on the Mirror building some few hundred yards away.

At the time as an industry we thought we had an unanswerable case, proving that the tied house system, far from being against the public interest, produced the cheapest pub or café beer in Europe. It also produced the widest choice and facilities that were the envy of the rest of the world. It was true that six companies sold nearly 80% of the beer between them and that the other 70 or so brewing companies, including Vaux, competed for the rest. With the exception of David Thompson of Wolverhampton Brewery, the industry was united in defending the status quo. The report when it came out, after nearly two years of deliberation, was disgracefully accepted almost without question by the then Secretary for Trade, Lord Young, with the remark, 'Let's drink Champagne – we have got the Brewers!'

I wrote the following letter to *The Times* which was published as lead letter on July 20 1989 under the heading 'Flaw in process on Monopolies':

> From the Chairman and Managing Director of the Vaux Group
>
> Sir, Lord Young's acceptance of the detriments alleged in the Monopolies Commission report on the brewing industry (report,

July 11) raises disturbing questions. The commission has as quasi-judicial role, but its procedures for reaching decisions which affect billions of pounds of investments and thousands of jobs are grossly flawed.

The commission, when it is asked to investigate an industry, becomes in effect, prosecutor, jury, and judge, the defendants being the members of that industry. However, those defendants do not know the details of the charges against them until the report is published. Such publication is analogous to conviction and sentence, but is announced by the Secretary of State for Trade and Industry, who, under the Fair Trading Act, is the only appeal unless malevolence could be shown.

When, as happened to the brewers, the secretary of state says he is 'minded to accept' at the time of the announcement it is little wonder that the brewers felt disturbed.

The commission hears evidence from many quarters, but no evidence is tested by cross-examination and what is accepted appears, in the brewers' case, capricious. Thus, evidence from the Brewers' Society that pub prices in Britain compared favourably with overseas was never questioned in hearings, but dismissed in the report as unsubstantiated, while some of the wilder statements of consumerist organizations were treated as near-gospel.

When the report was published the brewers believed they had a complete answer to each of the alleged detriments found by the commission, but they had no means of putting these over as the secretary of state refused even to listen to suggestions that the findings of the commission might not be in accordance with the facts. As things stand, the same fate awaits the oil companies and the credit-card issuers, and no doubt, like the brewers, they will be subject, when their report is published, to a chorus of ill-informed criticism from the usual anti-industry sources as well as some who should know better.

The whole economy is affected by substantial changes to one part of industry. Before such changes are made on the basis of a commission report, that basis should be subject to judicial review. The commission should be restricted to investigation and formulation of charges. Its findings should then go to, say, the Restrictive Practices Court for adjudication. If found proved, then, and only then, should the secretary of state use his powers under the Fair Trading Act to order change. The law should be amended as a matter of urgency to this effect.

Yours faithfully,

PAUL NICHOLSON, Chairman and Managing Director,
Vaux Group plc.

I was on record at the time as saying that the recommendations would lead to exactly the opposite of what was intended with less choice, fewer pubs and customers paying more for their beer in the pub or club. Even though some of the proposals were watered down, the long-term consequences of the rest are that it is now three companies who control 80% of beer sales. That only two of the regional companies, Greene King and Wolverhampton, still brew beer. Mansfield, Marstons, Morlands, Camerons, Boddingtons and Vaux having all disappeared. Overall pub prices are higher while brewing margins have been squeezed. This is because middlemen, in the shape of companies such as Pubmaster and Enterprise, now cut out a third portion from the cake which previously was shared by two.

The words of Lief Mills in his dissenting report should have been heeded. They were 'Don't interfere with what you don't understand!' The public would certainly have benefited if the government had listened.

The after effects of the monopolies report were eventually a factor in the destruction of Vaux, although this was more because I failed in the end to persuade my colleagues to ride out the storm. Companies that have, particularly such as Greene King, Wolverhampton, Fullers and Youngs, are now prospering. Companies that have exited brewing such as Greenalls, now ironically called de Vere, and even Bass and Whitbread have not so far done any favours for their shareholders.

While the main businesses of Vaux in the eighties were brewing and pubs on the one hand, and hotels on the other, we had also built up our substantial off licence chain of over 180 shops and the scope of this business had been widened to include some 30 convenience stores.

In 1987 we converted one of the hotels acquired with Sheffield Refreshment Houses into a nursing home. This proved very successful and having dipped our toe in the water, we took a plunge so that some three years later, we had 22 homes and over 1000 beds. We went into nursing homes as a business which had many of the same characteristics as hotels, requiring similar skills in lodging and catering, although nursing was of course, an additional skill. The division was managed by Nigel Spencer, a former director of Swallow, who reported to Peter Catesby. We saw an expanding market from an ageing population, but 'Care in the Community' legislation led to a dramatic cut in Government funding. In spite of a growing need, the potential of this business did not materialize and we sold in 1996.

I described Vaux colloquially in the late eighties as being in the 'Booze and Snooze' business. 'Booze' consisted of beer, wines, spirits, pubs and off licences, while 'Snooze', was our hotel and our care home business.

The Thatcher era ended in 1990. It had been a great decade for Britain and also for Vaux. We had survived the seventies and the eighties, as an independent company against the forecasts of many pundits, and in 1990 I was emboldened to write in the annual report of a company soundly based for growth. In common with many other companies within the sectors in which we traded, achieving this in the nineties was to be a much more severe problem than anticipated. The decade had also seen a revolution in business thinking, which had not at the time led to the excesses which were to become a feature of the nineties and indeed into the new Millennium. Looking back from a personal point of view this was my most successful time.

I was involved in so many different activities at the time that it took longer than it should have for several of the problems of the nineties to sink in. Emboldened by our success in hotels, we had become rash. New luxury hotels in Bristol and Birmingham were a step too far, particularly as for the second time in my career I was caught out by a loosely drawn construction contract leading to a massive overrun. The lessons learnt in the sixties with the building of the Swallow Newcastle had been forgotten, and the true overrun at Bristol, taking into account our failure to achieve a sale of an adjacent office block, was closer to £35 million than £25 million, although not all of this was apparent on the accounts. Swallow profits fell between 1990 and 1991 from £16 million to £11.5 million, and it was not until 1995 that they recovered in cash terms, during which time a further £60 million had been poured in. These were very difficult times for all concerned, but I was determined that we should not cut our refurbishment standards, although we did make savings of over £1 million in operating costs, and we did towards the end of this recession have the confidence to acquire a hotel in Rotherham and a share of a hotel in Grantham.

When the Swallow profit collapse of 1991 occurred, we were able to plug some of the gap in profits by substantial pub acquisitions resulting from disposals by the national brewers. These disposals were induced by the Office of Fair Trading 'Beer Orders', which had resulted from Lord Young's acceptance of so much of the Monopolies Commission report. While the pubs we bought were by no means rubbish, they were bottom end, and thus cheap. They provided a good quick fix to an emergency situation. Our pub acquisitions increased beer and pub profits from £18 million in 1990, to £26 million in 1993.

It was not comfortable for me, for the first time in my career, to be reporting results which overall were behind the previous year's figures. The share price fell nearly 50% from a high, which was admittedly inflated by bid speculation. This had not however deterred myself and other directors from accepting options, which now sunk a long way under water, and in the case of the '88 options, never to surface before they expired in 1998. The 1989 options at over £3 did however come good, on the sale of the company, at a share price some 20% higher than its peak in the eighties.

Firefighting, cash conservation and damage limitation became my principal concerns. We were better placed than some, such as Queens Moat and Stakis, which were in much worse trouble. In the case of Queens Moat, they were let off onerous loan conditions. This enabled them to compete on an unlevel playing field with soundly financed companies, such as Vaux, who never caused their banks such problems.

It became clear in the early nineties that our wine and spirit retail business could not be developed further. We negotiated a good price when selling this to Greenalls. To reward Anthony Wood who skilfully handled this sale more or less unaided, I inflated his severance package with some of the fees we might otherwise have had to pay a corporate financier. I also recommended he became a non-executive director. Neither he nor I thought he might be acting Chairman one day, albeit for only a few months!

As a result of selling five smaller hotels in 1990, we had a substantial windfall profit, and I decided to use a portion of this to deal with a perennial problem for many companies. What to do about the many appeals and charitable causes that they are asked to support. I allocated a million pounds to a Vaux Foundation, which could form a buffer between the company and applicants. I was careful that the foundation remained under the control of the directors from whom its trustees were drawn. The main aim of the foundation, as of the company, was to help non-national causes, particularly in the North East and around Sheffield, or where it could be of direct public relations benefit to a particular Swallow Hotel. Sadly, I did not make any provision for the foundation to become independent if the company was taken over. Whitbread have found it something of a windfall, I believe that its independence could have been negotiated without penalty as part of the sale deal if the Swallow directors had been interested.

The Vaux foundation was formed at about the same time as new Community Foundations for Tyne and Wear and for Cleveland. It was able to give these foundations substantial support in their initial stages and later helped the County Durham Foundation get off the ground.

As Chairman and Chief Executive of Vaux it was much easier to talk to investors when things were going well, than when there were problems. We continued with our open days aiming to present the company 'warts and all'. The 25th open day was held in February 1997, preceded for the only time in the 25 years of its existence by a dinner for all participants. At this John Walters, one of the City's most experienced brewery analysts, spoke amusingly and nostalgically of his unique record in being the only person apart from myself who had attended every single one. The previous year we had held 'open day' in the south at our hotel in Bexleyheath, because we were advised that analysts and institutions were increasingly reluctant to come north. However attendance there was well down. It was much better for the 'silver' occasion next year back in the North.

For a number of the earlier years, open days more than fulfilled their objective of meeting institutional investors' information requirements. There were some within the industry who felt we gave away too much. In the seventies I was remonstrated with by Derek Palmar, Chairman of Bass for the embarrassment I caused him, and others, by revealing so many facts about my own company, covering matters he considered confidential in his own. In the eighties, and particularly when faced with takeover speculation, we realized that 'open day' had to be reinforced with visits to major shareholders, and later with results presentations to the press and analysts, at the time of interim and final results announcements.

Few Chairmen of public companies can really have enjoyed 'brokers' lunches' which, were a fashionable means of communicating with the City. They are indigestible occasions! Various brokers held these for Vaux. Usually I was on my own but sometimes I was supported by the Finance Director. The principal guest on these occasions is expected, between mouthfuls, to give an account of his company, avoiding, in theory, revealing 'price sensitive information', but of course the fellow guests, who are normally representatives of actual or potential institutional investors, are really only interested in gleaning such information. In the seventies such lunches were pleasantly liquid, but by the nineties in the much more aggressive situation that now prevails, they had become largely 'dry'. This made them even more of a trial!

I had always played a part in industry affairs and was flattered to be asked to succeed Ian Prosser as Vice Chairman in 1992, and Chairman in 1994, of what was then called the Brewers and Licensed Retailers Association, but was formerly the Brewers Society. Before me, the only son to follow a father in that position had been my father, Chairman in 1968, who followed his father Sir Frank Nicholson, who had uniquely had two spells as Chairman in the twenties and thirties.

Normally the Chairmen of the Brewers came from major companies in the industry. There were only three other Chairmen in my time from regional companies, Teddy Thompson of Wolverhampton, Ewart Boddington and Anthony Fuller.

My spell as Chairman was mainly taken up with trying to hold together an increasingly disparate industry. Most of the several million pound costs of the Association were born by the major brewing companies. At the time there were six of these each paying several hundred thousand pounds a year. They were understandably restless about this. Following the beer orders there were an increasing number of large non-brewer multiple pub owners some of whom were in membership but others not. There was also a group of smaller brewers who had set up their own organization, called the 'Independent Family Brewers of Britain'. They remained in the Association and numerically formed a majority, but only contributed less than 10% of the costs between them.

Most of the major brewers believed that remaining in the Association was sensible politically, in that while the public attitude to big brewers was hostile it was much more amenable towards the smaller brewer. There were benefits to the big brewers in not being too confrontational with their smaller brethren. However the big brewers had little need for some of the more costly elements of the Association which were proportionally of far more benefit to the smaller company and this was an increasing cause of tension.

There were a number of 'characters' among the smaller brewers such as John Young, the staunchly independent Chairman of Youngs Brewery in London, and Bobby Neame of Shepherd Neame who could be relied upon to prolong meetings with some maverick views. These often turned out to be right!

The Association had monthly meetings in a prestigious headquarters in Portman Square. Meetings were followed by sumptuous buffet lunches over which the real business tended to be done. After my time, Portman Square was abandoned and general meetings became quarterly. As a Vice President of the Association I am asked to the Annual General Meeting. I attended one of these recently held at the Headquarters of the Trade Union Congress. How some of the great figures of the industry such as Col Bill Whitbread or Lord Boyd must revolve in their graves at the thought of such a venue – and the lunch was lousy!

A major concern in my time was dealing with European regulations covering the 'tie' such as the so called 'Block Exemption' allowing brewers to tie the tenants of pubs they owned to selling exclusively their own products. I think it was John Major who described dealing with Europe as like wrestling with a greasy pig. We had to deal with an arrogant little Belgian Commissioner Monsieur Van Miert. In the end nothing much changed, but the amount of time and effort senior people in an industry have to spend dealing with such gentlemen, has filled many of those who have had such experiences, including myself, with a deep scepticism as to what we are doing in Europe. The matters we were discussing had little, or nothing to do with the free trade organization we voted for, all those years ago.

As Chairman I also had to deal with UK Ministers, particularly over beer duty, where it remained a major bone of contention between the Industry and the Government that rates were so much higher than on the Continent. Dealing with UK Ministers such as the Chancellor of the Exchequer, at that time Ken Clarke, was in many ways just as frustrating and unproductive as dealing in Europe.

The Brewers were fortunate in my time to be served by an

excellent director, Robin Simpson, backed by an able secretariat under Martin Rees. I had largely been responsible for Robin's recruitment, as I had come across him as Regional Director for the Department of Trade and Industry in the North. While he didn't suit all tastes in the Association, particularly as he was not a clubbable man, and could show his impatience with some of the more obtuse members, he had a bright intellect and was a real 'Whitehall Warrior', as a former minister described him. If we had had him as director during the Monopolies Commission Enquiry, the result might have been very different.

There were some nice perks of office, including representing the British Brewers at the annual conference of the International Medical Advisory Group (IMAG) set up by the main English speaking Brewers Associations of Britain, United States, Canada, Australia and New Zealand following a poisoning problem in America in the sixties. Its aim was to identify the true position on various alcohol related subjects particularly health, and public safety matters such as drink driving. I attended three such conferences in Sydney, Australia, Tucson, United States, and Vancouver, Canada.

The conferences were particularly interesting to laymen and the doctors who attended. I learnt that far from all drink being harmful and sinful, moderate drinking was positively beneficial. Also, it was a myth that red wine had any special beneficial effects. Evidence was given in one presentation that even 'alcohol free' days advocated by some doctors could be damaging, in that if someone has not had a drink in the previous 24 hours, a heart attack is (a) more likely, and (b) if it occurs, will be more severe!

I also became, for a time, a Vice President of the European Brewers Association and among memorable venues for their annual conference were Capri, and Kiruna in Northern Sweden in the land of the midnight sun.

Back at base, Vaux years of record profits fortunately recommenced in 1995 with the hotel recovery but a change in Government policy regarding care in the community led to a decision to sell that business. This was achieved in 1996 but at a disappointing price, leading to a loss against book value.

It was only in 1996 that profits from Swallow began to pull ahead of the Breweries. They had previously been ahead for one year only. That was in 1989. Over the years 1993 to 1998 the brewery profits had stagnated, oscillating between £25.8 million and £26.9 million It was this that led to increasing concern about whether we should continue in brewing. I believed at the time, and believe to this day, that a decision to exit brewing was short termist, and that if we had stuck with it, it would have come right, as indeed is happening to others who have stayed with brewing through lean times. We did debate the issue fully at our annual think-tank meetings in 1995, 1996 and 1997. At these I was able to convince the board to stick with brewing, but I suppose it should have been obvious that a new Chief Executive would see an exit as a necessary change of direction, although the final Vaux situation was unusual in the failure to make the change efficiently and competently as well as humanely.

While maintaining my belief that the Group's two main businesses 'booze and snooze' were a logical combination, I did suggest to the Board demerger as an option, with the existing managing directors becoming chief executives of the two demerged companies. Our advisors ran over the numbers but did not believe this would add value. With hindsight I should have pushed this, as while hotels would almost certainly have been taken over, there could still have been a beer and pubs business although this could also have been vulnerable to takeover. Even if this had occurred, I believe both breweries would still have been operating today, contributing positively to prosperity and employment in Sunderland and Sheffield.

As mentioned in the next chapter, the Group had in the spirit of the corporate governance climate engendered by the Cadbury and other reports appointed new non executive directors who were elected independently. While two of the three appointed may have been competent in their own right none of them were to show any feelings for the tradition and ethos of the company.

A wise friend and advisor commented to me after the debacle, that these appointments were probably my biggest mistake.

CHAPTER 10

Death of Vaux

IN 1996 HAVING BEEN Chairman and Chief Executive since 1976, I told the board that I would like to relinquish the role of Chief Executive when I became 60, but that I would like to continue as Chairman.

The non-executive directors, particularly the senior non-executive director Stephen Gibbs whose role in the saga was pivotal, strongly advised me that neither of the two divisional Managing Directors, Peter Catesby of Swallow Hotels or my brother Frank Nicholson who ran Vaux Breweries, were suitable for the role of Group Chief Executive and that we must look outside. I agreed with this advice. Peter Catesby I considered too old, and in any case for two years he had advocated the group exit brewing which I did not agree with. My brother Frank had many good qualities, but in the current climate, unless the brewery side had been performing extremely well, which it wasn't, the City and institutional shareholders, many of whom, as Graham Searjeant was to describe in an article on what had happened which he wrote on 8th April 1999, 'hate family dynasties with a passion that reminds you of Robespierre', would not accept him.

Following the Cadbury and Greenbury Reports, I had thought it was time for changes among the non-executive directors, all bar one of whom were long serving. Peter Vaux thus stood down in 1995. Anthony Wood had been due to go in 1996, but because of his trade knowledge, in a time of transition, I recommended he remain, while Anthony Pearson who had served on the board since 1977 left in 1997.

He shared with me a strong belief in the North East, and its importance to what Vaux was about. I did not realize until too late, that after the changes made, and particularly Anthony Pearson's departure, there were no non executives who shared my beliefs that a company's heritage is important and that 'shareholder value' means more than short term fixes.

As replacements, two new directors were recruited, neither of whom had previously been known to others on the board, although I expect corporate governance fanatics would object that the consultant who found them was Andrew Nicholson, my third brother. He had been with Vaux in the seventies. The new directors were, John Conlan, former Chief Executive of First Leisure, a mercurial Irishman with the charm of that race, but a strong personality used to getting his way. After the destruction of the breweries, Sir Alick Rankin former Chairman of Scottish and Newcastle told me, shortly before he died, how difficult he had found Conlan to do business with, to the extent that he had stopped trying to deal with him. The other was Judy Atchison, then with the Halifax, currently with Whitehead Mann. She impressed initially with her marketing skills and strategic outlook but seemed overawed when it came to financial matters, and followed the lead of others through the process that led to the tragedy.

In the late eighties I had agreed with Peter Buckley, a member of the Cayzer family and Chairman of Caledonia Investments who were substantial shareholders, that they should suggest a director. Their earlier choice was Sir David Kinloch Bt who was very compatible. When he was unable to continue because of other commitments, I accepted Jonathan Cartwright who was their Finance Director and had previously been with the Hanson Group. He was like myself a member of the Institute of Chartered Accountants. Initially he appeared quite good, but when the crunch came he was not, in my view, up to the task he was asked to perform.

Thus of our five non-executive directors at the end of 1997 the majority, being Cartwright, Conlan and Atchison were 'independent' in the corporate governance sense.

At two board strategy sessions held in 1996 and 1997 a case had been presented by Tim Walker then Neal Gossage, successive finance directors, supported by Peter Catesby, to exit brewing, but on both occasions I had shown that in my view the numbers supported continuing brewing, and had persuaded the board albeit with some reservations to continue regional brewing. We did look at demerger of the two sides of the business. Peter Catesby was against, fearing a demerged Swallow Hotels would quickly be bid for, while calculations from our advisors showed, apparently, no great shareholder value increment at that particular time. The idea was therefore shelved and the board felt we should await a new chief executive and see what his strategy would be.

It was against this background that my then colleagues and I held a beauty parade of head-hunters and selected Heidrich and Struggles. They came up with one excellent candidate but unfortunately after protracted discussions, he decided to go elsewhere, and indeed has since gone on to be a high profile chief executive of a much larger company, where he has been very successful. Heidrich produced a number of candidates but for one reason or another they did not fit the bill. We therefore decided to change head-hunters and selected GKR. They came up with Martin Grant, a tied trade director at Allied Retail, a subsidiary of Allied Domecq. While I had some reservations about him, particularly when he said he would not move his home to the region, GKR claimed to have checked his references and he was offered the job in April 1998 with a putative start date later in the year. Heidrichs told me, after I had left the company, that they had considered Grant, but not thought him suitable to put forward.

In May of 1998 I received a call from the Chairman of Stakis proposing a 'friendly take-over' subject to being allowed due diligence. My board advised we must look at this. Stakis did not want the approach to become public unless the Vaux Board would recommend an offer. Inevitably when any approach involves City institutions there was a leak, the share price moved up 10% and the stock exchange required the Board to announce the existence of an approach.

The new Directors particularly John Conlan felt that Hambros our main London Advisors, who at that time were going through the Andrew Regan affair, were no longer suitable to be our corporate advisors, and persuaded the Board, against my better judgement, that we should seek a change. However, the Board did agree to retain our long serving joint advisor Noble Grossart, a distinguished Scottish firm, but sometimes resented among certain London institutions. Alongside them a firm called BT Alex Browne (BTAB) was selected. BTAB's subsequent performance in the Vaux Tragedy was critical to what happened.

Because of the approach, Martin Grant managed to obtain early release from Allied and joined the company in June 1998. In the meantime, talks between Stakis and Noble Grossart did not reveal the likelihood of an acceptable bid and discussions were terminated. There was inevitably a lot of tension and pressure within the board following the approach, and a new chief executive alongside new advisors with possible new ideas, was going to receive a very sympathetic hearing.

The only idea he could come up with was that we should close the breweries and buy from outside suppliers for our pub estate. The new advisors produced some specious, but to the non-executive directors mouth-watering numbers of what this might achieve. These put most of the board in no mood to listen rationally to arguments to the contrary.

Grant's advice may have been coloured by his experience at Allied, where Carlsberg Tetley had been given a very favourable supply agreement to the Allied Estate when Carlsberg had bought Allied's Breweries. Grant felt that this had wrongly reduced the pub profits he was responsible for at Allied retail.

Faced with Grant's advice I looked at other options which might at least save the breweries from closure. Two were emerging. The first was a management buyout, and this had the major attraction of preserving something of what Vaux had been about for the 150 years of its existence. The second followed an approach to me from the Chairman of Whitbread, who said that they would like to acquire Vaux if the board would recommend a bid. If they did, they would intend retaining the Sunderland brewery, but would have to find a home for Wards brewery which they would not keep. Possibly they would seek to sell to management as they had recently done with the nearby Castle Eden brewery in County Durham. Grant was on holiday at the time. I discussed the approach with the non-executive directors, and it was decided to give Whitbread similar information to what had been given to Stakis. However, they withdrew largely because the Vaux share price was so volatile following the earlier approach.

The proposed management buyout was led by my brother, Managing Director of the Group's breweries division. Because of the family connection, I had the choice of either resigning as Chairman to join his team, or if I remained as Chairman, I would have to distance myself from any decisions or negotiations concerning the terms of the buyout. I elected to do this, but it quickly became apparent that the new Chief Executive was very opposed to retaining the breweries, and was prepared to use almost any means to frustrate their survival. I found it impossible to discuss these issues rationally with him and from then on there was a near total breakdown of relations between us.

The issue of my lack of confidence in him came to a meeting of a committee of the non-executive board members in August 1998. The non-executives under the chairmanship of the longest serving non-executive director Stephen Gibbs interviewed myself and the other executive directors of whom Peter Catesby as well as my brother backed my view that Grant was not suitable to continue. However the committee decided to back him. Gibbs told me that this was the unanimous view not just of the non-executives but also all the executives. I knew this not to be true, but it was not to be the only misrepresentation he was to participate in as events unfolded.

I knew that if I resigned at that time, the breweries would certainly close, as none of the non executives were numerate so far as brewing was concerned, while I had less and less confidence in the competence of the new advisor the others were so mesmerized by. If I went, it would remove the only impediment between the Chief Executive and his aim of closing the breweries.

The Board with the exception of Grant and Neil Gossage the

finance director, at that stage, may have genuinely wanted to save the breweries if possible, but they were apprehensive that any deal with management would be criticized in the City, so they opted to put the breweries and sufficient pubs to make the package attractive, up for sale by open tender. The process of actually putting the package together proved protracted because of the lack of co-operation from the Chief Executive, to the degree that the non executives asked Peter Catesby to mediate, and it was he who decided what package of breweries, pubs and supply terms to the ongoing estate should be put out to tender. This was endorsed by the board and published with required offers by 30 November 1998.

Over the next two months the Chief Executive was in Sunderland less than half the time. He was not apparently looking at the rest of the business. I never did discover what he was up to. By this time there was a total breakdown of relations between us.

During that time I decided that in the longer term it would be wrong for me to remain as Chairman with a Chief Executive whom I could not relate to. I therefore told Stephen Gibbs privately, as the senior non executive director, before telling the board formally, that it would be my intention to retire when a suitable successor could take over. Gibbs asked that he should lead the process of finding the new Chairman to which I agreed as at the time I still trusted him. I anticipated that the process would take some months, during which time the breweries issue would be resolved.

The next I knew was a circular from him, only copied to me, excluding me from any part in the process of finding my successor. When I wrote to him remonstrating somewhat bitterly about this, he gave the excuse that the headhunter he was proposing to use had advised that it was normal to exclude an outgoing Chairman from such a process in circumstances where the company was changing direction – what rubbish!

When the deadline for offers passed, while there were bids for parts of the package from Mansfield Breweries and Carlsberg Tetley, the only offer for the whole including both breweries was from the management who, supported by a Venture Capitalist, Alchemy Partners, bid £75.5 million cash. The proposed management buyout was led by my brother Frank, Managing Director of the Group's Breweries division. He was supported by three of his Brewing Directors – Stuart Wilson, who oversaw all production, Doug Trotman, the Breweries Marketing Director and Mark Anderson, their Financial Director. There had been discussion with a number of parties, particularly Pubmaster, but they had decided to withdraw from a possible offer for the pubs part of the package. Faced with only one offer for the whole package, Grant persuaded the rest of the board that the management offer must be tested against the possibility of closure and a supply agreement with national brewers. At the same time he forbade any further negotiations with the management.

The supply terms in the management's offer were then hawked around the national brewers and a competitive frenzy between Bass, Whitbread and Carlsberg developed. Nothing further in the meantime was heard from Pubmaster.

This process culminated in January 1999, when, on the basis of the offers from the national brewers, Grant submitted a paper prepared in conjunction with BTAB, claiming that he could achieve up to £24 million more value for shareholders by closing the breweries and retaining all the pubs, rather than accepting the management offer.

It was only then that I was shown the calculations behind this claim and realized that the numbers were totally absurd. I prepared a paper showing that actually the management was still, albeit marginally, the better option in value terms, before attempting to quantify the damage to goodwill closure would cause.

By that stage the decision on these matters had been delegated to a committee of the Board chaired by Jonathan Cartwright who with his financial background was considered most appropriate to interpret the numbers. At an earlier stage Grant and Catesby had been on the committee but both had been removed because they were continually at loggerheads (Grant had however persuaded Catesby to take early retirement scheduled for the end of March

1999). The committee accepted in principle my position and authorized continued negotiations with management. This was approved at a board meeting on 15th January where for the first time in my career a formal vote was called for at which Grant and Gossage dissented from the decision. This was some two weeks before the 1999 AGM was due to be held and in the intervening period the negotiations continued to be fraught as Grant was so hostile. The day before the AGM I did not know which way the decision would go and had prepared two statements, one announcing that the MBO was being granted a period of exclusive negotiation, and the other announcing my resignation if this was not going to happen.

In the intervening period BTAB notified the board that Pubmaster, who had earlier withdrawn, had come back with an indicative offer of £40 million for the pubs in the original package, which on the surface looked a better alternative than straight closure retaining all the pubs. Grant and Gossage promptly changed their view and recommended Pubmaster's indicative offer. I was very suspicious of why this offer had materialized at the time it did, and remain so in the light of subsequent events. What was the role of BTAB in the matter, particularly as they insisted that the board must consider this approach even though it was received well after the deadline for closure of offers?

Coming up to the Annual General Meeting there was stalemate, but the fact that this could be highly embarrassing for the committee at the AGM which I would be chairing, spurred Cartwright into concluding an agreement with the management for a so called, 'period of exclusivity', minutes before the meeting was due to start. I was then able to announce this rather than my resignation. It was not an easy AGM particularly as Grant the Chief Executive sat glowering beside me. I fended off questions about his position.

At the 22 Annual General meetings I had chaired up to 1998, I had always discouraged a vote of thanks to the Chairman, mindful of the late Sir James Woodeson's description of this as one of the 'three most useless things in the world'. In case I offend my readers I will not mention what the other two were as they were somewhat ribald.

However at the 1999 meeting, before I realized what was happening, John Ward stood up. He started by saying how relieved he was at the announcement I had made earlier in the meeting. He then went on to make some flattering remarks about my years with the company during which profits had risen from £2 million to £41 million and also my role in the wider North East. He concluded . . .

> I promised not to embarrass him and I won't. I could spend half an hour detailing his achievements both within and without this Group, but I won't. But one final point please, because it is important to me, the business world has changed tremendously over the years and we all know Paul's qualities, but two stand out in my mind and always will. Ladies and Gentlemen, your Chairman cares, he cares about this Group, he cares about the City of Sunderland, which he loves, and he cares about the people of the North East. And secondly, his personal code of ethics I find unsurpassed, he has an integrity, Ladies and Gentlemen, in the business world which I again have found unsurpassed. Those are the two comments, I hope I have not embarrassed you Paul. Ladies and Gentlemen, I do hope you will join me in saying just two words to your Chairman – Thank you!

Vaux AGMs were traditionally social events attended by several hundred small shareholders, followed by a liquid buffet lunch. Immediately after the meeting Grant and Gossage left without mingling with shareholders. My statement had of course been positive about the management buyout, expressing my belief in this. Our City Public Relations Advisors wanted to issue this and indeed would have, but Cartwright actively supported by Gibbs sought to overrule me and instructed the somewhat bemused advisors that this should not be put out. It did not make much difference as I put it out on the internet through a website set up independently by outside friends of the brewery called 'Save Our Breweries'.

For a few days after that things were ominously quiet. I decided to see the largest shareholder Phillips & Drew whom I was reasonably close to, to explain the background to the current situation. I was informed that Grant had also made an appointment to see them.

On about 7th February 1999 Cazenove informed Cartwright, who then directly rang me, to say that, behind the backs of the board, Grant and Gossage had apparently approached major shareholders claiming the decision to grant the management a period of exclusivity had not been properly considered and they did not support it.

I called a meeting in London of those directors available which Grant and Gossage were told to attend. The meeting was held on 9th February. I had taken advice from our lawyers Slaughter & May and it was agreed that, should Grant and Gossage have done this, they must go. They made little attempt to deny they had done this. I think they were unaware of a provision I had had put in our articles in 1976, that were an executive director to be dismissed from his executive duties, he ceased to be a member of the Board, and they were thus somewhat surprised to find themselves no longer directors. I also recommended to the board that Peter Catesby who had been due to retire early, on 31st March following, because he could not work with Grant, should be appointed Chief Executive, with a two year contract, and this was accepted.

While originally I had not considered Peter suitable to be Chief Executive of the company as it was then structured, he had the necessary skills to run the ongoing Swallow Group with its primary focus on hotels. I knew there had been a degree of rivalry and antipathy between him and Frank but I believed this had subsided as both had supported my position in regard to Grant, although in their case as they reported to him rather than me they had to use a degree of circumspection.

I had high hopes at this time that, while there would be a fair amount of flak on the matter, the way should now be cleared for a sensible deal with the management buyout team, which I was convinced, was a better long term alternative to shareholders than closure. Sadly within six weeks these hopes were to fall apart.

However I thought at the time that at last the Board had experienced themselves the problems I had been having with the Chief Executive, which in my view, made him the wrong man for Vaux, a view I had repeatedly expressed to them over the preceding months. Although Gibbs wrote a sycophantic letter to my wife hoping to 'restore relationships with Paul', he and the others actually seem to have resented the fact that I might have been right about my problems with the Chief Executive.

At the meeting where Grant and Gossage were dismissed it was agreed that explanations would have to be given to City shareholders and that the best people to do this were Jonathan Cartwright and John Conlan, who were the only two directors apart from myself with substantial city connections and were also clearly independent.

The reactions of some elements of the press, particularly Lex in the *Financial Times* and certain of the Sundays, were cynical and scathing about me and my relationship with my directors. Some shareholders were also hostile, preferring to believe what they had been told by Grant and Gossage, although the more responsible did accept that for two directors to go behind the backs of their colleagues made their position untenable. Several shareholders stated they would vote against any deal with management, unless the board could convince them that, in the then brewing climate, with perceived overcapacity throughout the industry, a deal with management really was in the interests of the company. Pressure from the press and these shareholders forced Wood and Gibbs to come off the sale committee, because they were not in corporate governance terms 'independent'. This left the three directors, who actually knew least about the breweries as the only members, because they were the only directors perceived to be independent.

The sale committee was, throughout this period, being fed with calculations from BTAB showing apparent benefits of closure up to £15M ahead of the management's offer. In calculating these, BTAB assumed very optimistic profit improvement projections from alternative supply agreements, with the brewery closed, of up to £14 million over five years. They also assumed that an asset strip of the breweries would yield a net £31 million. I repeatedly warned them that these numbers were wrong, but it was difficult for me because of the reluctance on behalf of BTAB and the committee actually to show me the numbers. The negotiations with the management and Alchemy, their backers, became increasingly fraught, largely because there was no clear line of authority and decision-making. Peter Catesby as Chief Executive might agree a point only to have it overruled by Cartwright or Conlan. Cartwright as the supposed financial expert was Chairman of the Sale Committee and in nominal charge. He simply could not see the wood from the trees. He kept getting hung up on what should have been non-issues, such as trying to insist that the MBO should both take over the creditors and pay full cash for the stock and debtors, instead as in any normal business sale paying for the net working capital.

He, together with the advisors and the committee, tried to insist on a totally unacceptable 'clawback' provision in case the MBO ever sold on parts of the sites. The affect of this would have meant among other things that had the MBO not been successful, there would have been no resources for redundancy. These were some of the issues which illustrate the confrontational way in which negotiations with the MBO and their backers were conducted.

The directors were extremely twitchy about city reaction, particularly following a letter from that self appointed cheer leader for Corporate Governance Alastair Ross Goobey of Hermes. After a visit from Conlan, he wrote stating 'The concerns we expressed about the current composition of the board and the sale committee would make it highly unlikely that we would support an MBO on the terms outlined'.

The whole negotiations descended into a mess, until on 17th March Cartwright phoned me to say negotiations were becoming bogged down and could I do anything to help. I then arranged for the MBO team and their advisors to meet the company's advisors on 18th March to try to resolve matters in advance of the Board meeting scheduled for 19th March. On the evening of 18th

March, I had dinner with Cartwright and Gibbs at the Royal County Hotel, Durham, at which I was led to believe that things had gone well and a deal was going to be done.

The next day the whole Board were present at a meeting in the head office in Sunderland, except for Anthony Wood, who was racing at Cheltenham and John Conlan who would take part on a conference line. The two advisors BT Alex Browne and Noble Grossart were also on a conference line as was Cazenove.

After dealing with routine business which I chaired, I handed over the chair to Cartwright, chairman of the sale committee, but was invited to stay in the meeting, as were all the other directors present.

The advisors were then invited to state their advice, which I was firmly expecting to be positive. David Mathewson of Noble Grossart advised that a deal looked possible, but then the representative of BTAB said that their advice was that the management's final offer was not acceptable. Noble Grossart subsequently told me that they were as surprised as I was at this advice, because it was not how they thought the position had been left the night before. Roger Lambert of Cazenove then advised that without agreement between the corporate finance advisors, shareholders were unlikely to support a deal.

BTAB had faxed to the meeting a latest version of their calculations which I summarize in Appendix 1. They claimed that following offers of supply terms from each of the National Brewers, and offers for parts of the original package from Mansfield Brewery and Pubmaster, there were ten alternatives for the Board to consider delivering between £8.6 million and £15.4 million more value than the management's offer. All the alternatives involved closure of Vaux Brewery in Sunderland although the Mansfield offer envisaged a temporary reprieve for Wards Brewery in Sheffield. The basis of all the alternatives was that the net realization from an asset strip of the Breweries would deliver £31.4 million.

I tried again to point out as I had repeatedly been doing over the preceding weeks, that their numbers were wrong, but BTAB were adamant in their advice to reject the management's offer. In the debate that followed it was clear that Conlan also on the conference line agreed with BTAB. I thought at the time that he must have had a hand in changing BTAB's advice because throughout the negotiations he had been ambivalent about a deal, considering that the proposed short term supply agreement was too generous to management. I don't believe now that this was actually the case, but I do know that BTAB's advice led, in due course, to what seemed to me to be a very favourable deal for Pubmaster whose finance it subsequently emerged, they were arranging. I do not know what connections there were if any between Pubmaster and BTAB at the time. BTAB refused to disclose to Chris Mullin, the Sunderland MP, when their relationship with Pubmaster had started, claiming 'client confidentiality' and in the press 'Chinese Walls'. A letter to the *Financial Times* pointed out later – that Chinese Walls are made of paper!

After their advice, I left the meeting to prepare one last appeal to the board not to take the closure route. However after I left the meeting the board then backed rejection of the management offer. The MBO team had been invited earlier to lunch with the board in expectations on both sides I believe that a deal would be done, however the lunch was cancelled!

I had been due to go to Windsor that afternoon to join Sarah who had motored down for a meeting of Lord Lieutenants that weekend. I had to phone her to ask her to return which she did leaving the car to be collected later. That weekend I went to see a close friend and advisor who was in full touch with events, he said that I should make my position clear to the board but warned that they did not appear to be in a listening mode. Nevertheless I faxed the paper (Appendix 2) to the whole board on Monday 22 March setting out why I believed that to reject the management offer was commercially unsound and therefore morally wrong. However on Tuesday 23rd March Peter Catesby announced to the Sunderland workforce that the management's offer was rejected and that the breweries would close on July 2nd unless a buyer emerged, which was about as likely by then as that pigs could fly.

The announcement was greeted with outrage across the North East, which sadly was to prove impotent in the face of a powerful city lobby and an intransigent board. It caused total shock and bewilderment among the hundreds of loyal employees in the breweries with tearful scenes being shown on television and reported in the local press.

Following my statement at the AGM eight weeks earlier and the subsequent departure of Grant and Gossage almost everyone working for the Breweries had expected a deal to be done. They thought they were working for an ethical company, which Vaux had prided itself in being down the years. In such companies there is normally a bias to seek solutions which while preserving shareholder value, avoid factory closures where the business can be sold instead.

I am afraid my then colleagues were far more influenced by opinion in the city press and institutions and belief in the incompetent numbers BTAB were peddling.

The decision they made as well as being based on numbers which I had repeatedly warned them were wrong, far from being tough was in my belief feeble. They were not prepared to face down their city Gods. I told them in my final memo (Appendix 2) any institutional shareholder revolt, would I believe have quickly evaporated. Who even among the most aggressive of these institutions, would have raised his head above the parapet to face the political and public heat that would have been turned on those wanting to throw hundreds of people out of work in the depressed cities of Sunderland and Sheffield. As I relate in a subsequent paragraph, even Hermes appeared to be starting to duck and weave when a bit of odium might have been coming their way.

I quickly dissented on television and in the press and may have used some intemperate language when accusing my colleagues of having 'lost their marbles' to one journalist, where I thought I was speaking off the record. My colleagues could sack me as Chairman but couldn't remove me from the board without a general meeting of the Company, as unlike Grant and Gossage I was not, at that time, executive. However on Thursday 25th March I realized that, while the local press was supportive of my stand, the national press was mainly hostile, and the city press overwhelmingly so. I thought that if I resigned, there was a remote chance of light rather than heat being generated and a deal being done. I also realized that remaining on the Board in such circumstances was unlikely to be good for the company I had led for so long. I therefore telephoned Gibbs the senior director and offered terms for my resignation, which were basically just to honour my one-year contract of £70,000.

There followed some rather silly moves to make me go at once, with a threat relayed to me by Catesby on my mobile phone while I was on a train to London, that if I did not agree to announce my resignation the next day, there would be an announcement that the directors were calling a meeting to remove me as Chairman and replace me with Anthony Wood.

I asked Gibbs for any announcement regarding my position to be delayed until after the upcoming weekend so as to give me time fully to prepare a resignation statement and inform people after my 23 years as Chairman.

He replied that he could not agree to this with the pathetic excuse that he was only the messenger. However by that stage the issue was becoming petty and not worth further argument. So on Friday 26th March 1999 I announced my resignation. This announcement was followed by a one from the company that Anthony Wood would be acting Chairman until a new Chairman could be appointed.

I found out two days later the hazards of not being discreet when on a train! The *Journal* newspaper ran a story repeated in the *Financial Times* of how I had been sacked. The storyline was that a fellow passenger on the train had overheard parts of my phone conversation and also remarks I made to Sarah who was with me, that they were trying to sack me.

There had been one moment of light relief when, on 25th March, I took a call from Mr Ross Goobey of Hermes, while I was on a train to London. He was upset on two counts, that he had been named in an adjournment debate in the commons by an

MP who had seen a copy of his letter to the board. He denied that this had been intended to influence the board! He was also upset that apparently this MP had been in touch with Trade Union trustees of Hermes funds to suggest that these trustees should tell the Hermes management to support sale of the breweries. He thought this was quite wrong. I did not actually comment at the time, that were not his trustees equivalent to shareholders, and should they not be allowed to exercise the same pressures on him, as he sought to do on companies in which he was invested? Some two years later I met him in another context and must admit I rather liked him but I believe he called it wrong at Vaux. The Hermes crusade for corporate governance would be more credible if they were more open with their own performance and their own senior executives did not appear to be such blatant 'fat cats'.

On the evening of the day the decision was announced, Cartwright telephoned Frank, full of unctuous sympathy, to say that his bid was £5 million short of what the board could accept. In a statement in the House of Commons Stephen Byers, then Secretary of State for Trade and Industry, stated that subject to conditions an additional £5 million might be available.

However, by then there was clearly a mindset for closure. The directors, hyped up by the belief, encouraged in sections of the financial press, that they must take the 'tough decision' were not open by then to rational argument.

The management team and their backers Alchemy Partners attempted to keep the door open and in a letter dated 31st March to BTAB they asked them to put forward three alternatives to the Swallow board. The third of which was worded 'a more radical approach which we would be prepared to explore with you' was to buy all the tenancies as well as the breweries but dropping any ongoing supply requirements to the rest of the group, in return for effectively doubling the original cash offer.

BTAB and the board did not even have the courtesy to reply to this letter before announcing through the press on the first of April that they were not prepared to reopen negotiations. Of course after closure was announced the value of the business sank rapidly as competitors moved in to win Vaux's customers.

I could not and would not have taken the stand I did, had I believed the numbers on the basis of which my colleagues were rejecting the management bid were credible. I accept that companies are not charities. If the economic case for a decision to throw hundreds out of work is sound, then it is in the longer term counterproductive to keep people working in an uneconomic fashion. If I had believed the numbers were true, I would have sought to retire quietly but sadly, rather than resign furiously.

On 8th April 1999 barely a week after finally closing off the MBO, the Swallow Board probably, I would speculate, bamboozled by further superficially plausible numbers from BTAB, announced that they were putting all the Group's tenanted pubs up for sale. On 28th June they announced further that they had concluded an agreement subject to shareholders approval for a sale of these to Pubmaster. At around the same time it became public that Pubmaster's funding was being arranged by the same BTAB.

I don't know when the Swallow Board became aware of BTAB's involvement with Pubmaster but I find it hard to believe that BTAB had no involvement with Pubmaster at the time the then surprising advice had been given on 19th March for closure of the breweries. Assuming of course that BTAB's advice was fully objective at all times, it was an extraordinarily satisfactory outcome for them. In the eighteen months during which they advised the Vaux/Swallow Board they managed to scavenge at least four sets of lucrative six or seven figure fees from the carcass of the company, three from the company itself and a further fee for arranging Pubmaster's finance for its purchase of the pubs.

Within the company the tenanted pubs division yielded a much higher return on capital than other parts of the business. An article in one of the local newspapers pointed out that the group was selling high yielding assets to invest in low yielding managed pubs or hotels. My calculations showed that the proposal as set out would lead to a dilution of over 20% on earnings. I therefore spoke out against the proposal at the Extraordinary General Meeting and also attacked the Board for what I believed was corporate vandalism in their decision to close the Breweries.

At the meeting itself various figures were produced by Peter Catesby, Chief Executive, which not being aware of in advance I was not able to challenge at the time. However these clearly showed that the numbers on which the closure decision had been based were already wrong, by some £12-15 million. Catesby also made a totally misleading statement that what had been achieved 'was £30 million better than management's final offer'. He put a 'spin' on the statement 'a more radical approach which we would be prepared to share with you' as a 'final offer'. No such final offer had been made, and indeed based on what Pubmaster had offered for the pubs in the original package compared to the additional amount they were prepared to offer for the other pubs they bought, Management's proposal would still have been a much better deal for shareholders.

A show of hands at the end of the meeting showed a large majority against the Board, but of course we all knew that from the point of view of any decision, the meeting was a sham, the Board already had the City institutions proxy votes in their pockets.

However, after the meeting, I wrote to Cartwright (Appendix 3) pointing out that on the basis of the numbers actually given at the meeting, those on which the Board had made their decision were already wrong by £10-15 million. An original estimate that a positive of £2.9 million would come from working capital was now revealed actually to be a deficit of £6 million, closure costs were now estimated at some £5 million higher than had been allowed for.

I received a pompous reply (Appendix 3B) which looked as if it had been largely drafted by lawyers. It avoided answering any of the specific points I had made, claiming 'Judgemental areas... will only be proven in the light of future events'. It was full of bluster about how the board regarded my 'unfounded criticism' very seriously. It alleged that I was implying other than honourable conduct by the Board and that I was conducting some sort of campaign which was against the interests of the company and its past and present employees. Neither of these allegations were true.

However part of his complaint was certainly correct. My letter did indeed imply questions about the competence of the Board and the integrity of BTAB's financial model. Cartwright and his colleagues obviously resented being reminded that, while I was still with the company, I had repeatedly warned them the numbers they were working on were very flawed.

I could only reply that he had failed to address any of the substantive points in my original letter and went on '. . . of the criticism of your actions you read into my letter, some were not made, the rest are very well founded on the facts . . .' I concluded 'you refer in your final paragraph to an alleged campaign. There is no such campaign. The closure of the Breweries is history. The value destroyed and the misery caused can now rest only on the commercial and social consciences of those responsible.'

Ironically in view of the criticism I had faced from the financial press I was invited by a gathering of brewery analysts from the City to a lunch on 26th May 1999 to thank me for my help to them over my years in the saddle at Vaux. Apparently they had only previously held such an event for chairmen of major companies in the industry and never before for the chairman of a regional company. There were 16 there, led by John Walters, Philip Shaw and Neil Scourse and they made a presentation of some attractive racing prints, which today hang in my office. I was also made a presentation by Sunderland Football Club in thanks for Vaux's support over the years, and by the *Journal* newspaper, but most treasured of all was a tankard given to me by four ladies from the bottling hall and cleaners Teresa Hutchinson, Brenda Hodgson, Irene Ross and Jean Orwin, in thanks for keeping them in employment for so long. Not surprisingly no form of memento came from the Company to mark my time at the helm.

During the weeks leading up to the actual closure there was naturally a lot of public interest. Probably the most emotional event was a service of thanksgiving for Vaux Breweries held at Sunderland Minster on 22nd June, when the Bishop of Durham gave a moving address which brilliantly encapsulated so much of what Vaux had been about. The full address is in Appendix 4.

He started with some amusing comments on the irony of a Bishop of Durham speaking at a thanksgiving service for a Brewery, going on to comment that until very recently you could be warmed or powered by Sunderland coal, look through a lens made from Sunderland glass and travel in a ship built on the Wear. With Vaux beers he said 'you could savour the taste of Sunderland'.

He pointed out that there was nothing unchristian about wealth for the common good but that going for the largest profit at the price of justice and the common good or for personal greed was wrong.

He did not seek directly to condemn what had happened, but pointed out that what those in power do, must be done in utter fairness and with an eye to the needs of others and their rights as human beings.

He paid tribute to what had been the ethics of Vaux in looking after the people who worked for the company and also went on 'In the Vaux and Sunderland context, I must express the great debt that we all owe to several generations of the Nicholson family. It was them who not only built up a successful business, but made sure that its breweries had a caring and family atmosphere about them. Many of the people who work in Vaux have counted it a privilege to do so simply because they have caught the inspiration and the fair-minded leadership of successive generations of Nicholsons. Moreover, the spirit has been made infectious and I have been glad to meet a number of people working at Vaux who are themselves the current expression of their own long family traditions. Not only have skills been passed down from generation to generation, but an understanding of the way in which Vaux works and in which it has succeeded not only in building, but one which it was good and enjoyable to work for.'

Vaux site under demolition, 2002.
(Photo courtesy of The Sunderland Echo.)

He concluded with the hope that whatever was to happen to the site would be worthy of its history and its importance to the City of Sunderland.

In this context as the site picture shows nearly four years on, it is an eyesore and while there is a visionary scheme produced by the Urban Regeneration Company, the practicalities may mean that it will finish as mainly accommodating a superstore shed.

After closure a sale of all loose assets such as furniture, stable equipment, glass etc was announced to be held on September 10th. When the catalogue came out, I suppose it was not surprising to find that the five remaining Vaux Breweries gold tankards, left over from the days of racing sponsorship, were not in the sale, they were apparently worth about £6,000 each. I had authorized in my time that we should not dispose of these, in case we changed back our sponsorship policy, but in the meantime some had been given as leaving presents to certain directors. It was also surprising and disturbing to find that certain assets, which clearly belonged to my family, were included in the sale. It took the threat of an injunction to get these back. Included also in the sale were such items as stable men's liveries, which the company had refused to pass onto those who wore them, and a number of other items which were very personal to individuals who had used them.

The stopgap Chairman, Wood, had been an executive director running our comparatively small off licence division until we had sold this in 1991. I had at that time recommended that he be offered a Non Executive Directorship, because I felt a degree of loyalty to a colleague from the North East during what was a difficult time for him, having had his job sold from under him.

Wood had told me during the weeks between Grant's departure and my resignation that the other directors had had a contingency plan to appoint him to fill the gap if I was to resign prematurely. He was apparently the only volunteer on the board for such a position.

He was probably only a bit player in the actual decision to close the breweries but as Chairman was active in executing that decision. Frank told me how Wood and Catesby had made veiled threats against him about his likely terms of severance in order to try and gag him during the weeks leading up to the actual closure.

Wood was replaced as Chairman in August 1999, after some five months in the Chair, accepting one of the Vaux Breweries gold tankards as his reward for his contribution to the destruction of those breweries.

The new Chairman was a Mr George Greener who had formerly been with Hillsdown Holdings. Apart from what appeared in the 1999 final accounts I know little about him. I never met him and the one letter I wrote to him went unanswered.

Greener came into a company which by then was directionless and floundering but an obvious candidate for a bid. I gather the directors had tried to merge with de Vere (formerly Greenalls), but it was a relief to all concerned when Whitbread, who had earlier expressed strong interest particularly in Swallow Hotels, returned with an offer that put the company out of its misery, albeit leading to the loss of several hundred more jobs. It may have been coincidence, but a few weeks before the announcement of Whitbread's recommended offer, I asked a close friend, who also knew well the then chairman of Whitbread, Sir Michael Angus, to tell him how vulnerable the company now was, which my friend duly did.

The offer from Whitbread, while not particularly generous if so much value had not already been destroyed, was nevertheless at a price substantially higher than the share price had ever been and some forty times the low of the 1970s when I first took charge.

Somewhat to my surprise the board did publish accounts for the year to September 1999. These came out after the bid from Whitbread had been announced. There was no date set in these accounts for an AGM as the board assumed that this need never be held. They would have faced some awkward questions had they had to face such a meeting. I set some of these out in a paper dated February 2000 which I called 'Postscript to the Demise of Vaux'. I sent this to those directors primarily responsible. The only written response was from Cartwright's office unsigned by him enclosing a further copy of his August 1999 piece of pomposity (Appendix 3B).

The 1999 accounts revealed that the shortfall against the figures on which the closure decision had been based was already £12 million, assuming the Brewery sites in Sunderland and Sheffield fetched what had been estimated. It also became apparent that the cost of an early retirement offer taken up by some 120 employees, had not been revealed, but was taken against an assumed pension fund surplus. The true shortfall before property was thus at least £15 million.

Hiding costs in the pension fund was not the only deception in the accounts. Page 39 contained a so-called 'restated' segmental analysis of the profitability of different sections of the business. This purported to show that the breweries had been loss-making in 1998 as well as in 1999 with an implication that this situation had existed for some years. I asked the auditors how they could explain verifying such a restatement. They replied that they had not done so. The accounts of 1998 and earlier had a segmental analysis as is normal in a public company, and this had been covered by the auditors' report. However nowhere in the 1999 report was attention drawn to the fact that page 39 was not covered by their report. I do not believe that one person in a hundred would have noticed this. It seems that a compromise had been reached between the board and the auditors because of the by then certain acquisition of the company.

The restated segmental analysis was nonsense, but part of the general attempt to direct attention away from the overall incompetence of what had happened. It was based on a retrospective change of the transfer prices between the breweries and Vaux pubs. In Vaux accounts for 1998 and earlier years the transfer prices used were actually lower in general than those common in the industry. The restated prices if applied across the industry as a whole would have meant that every pub-owning brewery would have shown a loss on their brewing operations. Vertical integration was still a key element of the brewing industry in 1999.

At the time of the takeover there was one fig leaf left, which the likes of Cartwright, Gibbs and the rest of the gang who destroyed Vaux believed would cover up their poor judgement. At a meeting I had in January 2000 with Catesby and the Swallow Finance Director Tim Walker, they admitted that there was a large shortfall in what had been realized so far as against what the BTAB model had predicted, but they stated that most or all of this would be made up because the Brewery sites in Sunderland and Sheffield would be sold for far more than had been allowed for. They told me that the Sunderland site alone which had been valued in the model at £10 million was likely to be sold for well over £20 million.

The Sheffield site was indeed sold shortly after the takeover for £1.4 million more than the numbers in the model. However the Sunderland site sat on the market for two years while Whitbread attempted to sell it. During that time they started to demolish the buildings then stopped apparently because of asbestos problems, leaving a terrible eyesore in the heart of Sunderland. Finally in 2002 they announced that they had sold the site to Tesco, the price was not disclosed but there is reliable information that it fetched around £12 million. There was a small piece of land apparently not included in the sale. Allowing for this, the total value Whitbread will have realized from the Sunderland site is unlikely to have been more than £13.3 million and may well have been less.

The sale of the Sunderland site virtually completed the disposal of the Brewery assets. An analysis of Swallow's statutory accounts for the years 2000 and 2001, which had to be prepared for debenture holders, showed further under recoveries and extra expenses from the closure. I prepared a paper in March 2002 (Appendix 5) where I have been able to make a comparison between the BTAB model and the out turn using the same discount for time factors as were in that model. While it is not possible to get audited figures, I am confident my numbers are overall on the conservative side.

BTAB's model had estimated that the asset strip of the Breweries would yield £31 million. It actually yielded around £16 million. BTAB had also assumed what I believe were highly optimistic profit improvement projections in their paper purporting to claim the benefits of closure were up to £15 million greater than the management offer. As these profit projections cannot be disproved, I have not attempted any adjustment to these in my comparisons of the out turn with the estimate. Catesby had claimed at the extraordinary general meeting held in July 1999 for the sale of the tenancies, that the Board would have accepted the management offer if the gap between closure and acceptance had been less than £10 million because of the unquantifiable damage to goodwill closure would cause. The final figures show that the management offer was at least as good as the closure alternative and almost certainly would have turned out better for the group and its shareholders. If those responsible had shown a modicum of competence, 500 jobs would not have been wantonly destroyed in the depressed cities of Sunderland and Sheffield.

I sent copies of my comparison paper (Appendix 5) to those responsible pointing out that the 'future events' in Cartwright's letter of August 1999 (Appendix 3B) were now in the past. The covering letter to Cartwright suggested his company, Caledonia Investments, might make a donation to the communities of Sunderland and Sheffield from the millions they had made from the sale of the group following his mistake. This time there was no response! A friend with a close connection with Sunderland followed this up with a letter to Peter Buckley, Cartwright's chairman at Caledonia, making a similar suggestion. Buckley told my friend when they happened to bump into each other that he was thinking about his letter but his thoughts have not so far been productive (April 2003)! The only response I received was from Anthony Wood who while making no apology did have the decency to admit that the board may have been wrong.

So what happened to the four remaining Vaux Breweries Gold Tankards? Apparently these ended up in the hands of the Gibbs and the three executive directors. What a fitting prize for their part in the destruction of those breweries!

Whitbread quickly sold on the bulk of the managed houses and put up for sale the 12 bottom end Swallow Hotels, although so far (April 2003) without finding a buyer. What was a successful independent North East company has been smashed asunder, but at the end of the day the takeover bid by Whitbread has at least realized value for the shareholders if one is of the fashionable belief that a board's duty is to maximize short term value by break up and sale.

It was unfortunate that the approach from Stakis occurred when it did. It caused the new chief executive to join earlier than originally intended and in a highly charged atmosphere. The board, by now dominated by the new non-executives, could not accept my reasons for quickly losing confidence in the new chief executive. It was particularly distressing that the senior non executive Gibbs, who I thought had been my friend and confidant for 26 years, for reasons best known to himself went along actively with the betrayal of all Vaux had stood for. It is distasteful that in seeking to justify his conduct, he has sought to claim to family and friends that the board had received a unanimous recommendation from the advisors to reject the management's offer on 19th March 1999 and therefore they could not have acted differently. This was simply not true. If I had had an ounce of support from him during the months leading up to my resignation, the tragedy at Vaux might have been averted. It was a particular irony that this individual had married my wife's sister. Press criticism of his position, as being too close to me, could not have been wider off the mark.

I finish this chapter with a quote from a letter from Alan Ogden a former Public Relations Advisor to the Group: 'I have only vaguely picked up on events at Vaux, but it did seem all a great shame. What struck me was that the values the company had worked so hard to instil and live up to – transparency, openness, believing in people, care of the community – all seemed to be sacrificed on the grubby altar of spurious shareholder value'.

Epilogue

LIFE MOVES ON. There is little to be gained from crying over spilt milk. Sarah and I have adapted to a new way of life rather earlier than had been intended. She reminds me that being married for life does not mean being married for lunch. Rather too frequently she has not just me but my part time PA Sanchia Coatsworth as well.

There are of course compensations. One learns who are one's real friends and Sarah and I have many of these. When my morale was rather low after the Vaux debacle, it was lifted by being asked by David Johnson, owner of Steelite International, to join his board. This had been agreed with his other non-executive director Mark Cannon Brookes. Both of these had been friends for over 30 years.

While it is not politically correct to have friends on the board, in David's case he owned the company so could do as he liked.

Steelite is a great success story and David a true entrepreneur. He came from a Stoke-on-Trent pottery family but it was his own initiative and with the help of the banks that he bought Steelite out of Wedgewood in the early eighties and built it up into a world leader in the supply of crockery to the catering industry. He has recently sold the company to the management. Because of his success, he has been able to buy back a lovely estate which had once been in the Johnson family, Chartley in Staffordshire, famous for its herd of wild white cattle. He and his wife Virginia gave a most spectacular party in the ruins of Chartley Castle for his 60th birthday.

His other non-executive director, Mark Cannon Brookes, was one of the three founders of NCL Investments, now a leading private client investment manager. I had known him and his wife Nicky since well before they were married.

I was appointed to the Board of the Scottish Investment Trust (SIT) in 1998. As the only Englishman on its board, I keep reasonably in touch with what is going on, particularly as I am Chairman of their Audit Committee which, until September 2002, had Andersens as the Auditors.

SIT has been chaired for many years by Sir Angus Grossart, rated one of Scotland's most powerful men. It is unusual among investment trusts, in that the managers are employees concentrating solely on the affairs of the trust rather than coming from a management company, with a portfolio of different trusts.

Founded in the 1880s, it is one of the oldest trusts in existence. As a board we see ourselves primarily as servicing the needs of private shareholders by providing them with a vehicle to invest their savings across a wide range of international markets. However, as the shares are fully listed on the London stock exchange, a number of city financial institutions have built up stakes. Some of these institutions have been attracted by the fact that SIT's shares trade at a discount to the total underlying value of the investments SIT holds. A few institutions have tried to put pressure on the board to embark on exercises in financial engineering, splitting the capital into separate funds, which they claim would reduce the discount. I am glad to say that the board is firm in resisting such pressures, which would fundamentally change the company to something which would be very different from what our private shareholders thought they were investing in.

The Vaux tragedy is now history. I was able to save from the wreckage the Vaux coach horses, which are now established at Beamish Open Air Museum as a major attraction. I have an arrangement whereby I can have them for certain coaching events including the Royal Ascot Race Meeting.

Just before I had my final clash with my former Vaux colleagues, I received an invitation to give a lecture to the 'Bristol Society' on a subject of my choice. The Bristol Society members are apparently drawn from the 'great and the good' of Bristol and the South West. They invite several guest speakers each year to give a presentation.

Because of the traumas I was facing at the time involving business behaviour, I decided that my subject would be 'business ethics'.

I don't want to sound sanctimonious, but I do feel that there are serious problems with present day business ethics, and that the Vaux tragedy was to some extent a result of these.

In my speech at the Bank of England debate a decade earlier, I had commented then on my concerns, that if businesses were not perceived to be acting in the public interest they would actually in the longer term be destroying shareholder value, because in any democratic regime this would provoke damaging regulation and restriction.

When discussing business ethics in the context of public companies and what should be their relationships with their so-called stakeholders, there are two fundamentally conflicting philosophies. There is the Milton Friedman School, who hold that a business's sole duty is to make profit. He has said 'Businesses are in the business of maximizing shareholder value by a prudent use of scarce resources, as long as the activities of the business are within the letter of the law'. The other view which could be defined as the corporatist view, is that businesses should be managed for the benefit of their stakeholders be they customers, suppliers, employees and local communities as well as their owners, the shareholders. Disciples of this view believe that corporate leaders have a responsibility to all stakeholders.

My personal belief inclines me to the Friedman School, rather than the corporatist, with a major qualification, which is that we live in a democratic society. How we behave, or are seen to behave, can affect adversely or favourably towards us the behaviour of the stakeholders, who ultimately are responsible for our profits and shareholder value. Customers can be influenced favourably by the perception that the company whose products or services they are buying is a good citizen and supports the local community. They can be turned off by perceptions that a company is behaving badly.

More fundamentally, however, excesses of corporate behaviour lead to restrictive regulation and legislation. Raw capitalism 'à la

Friedman', exercised without sufficient regard to stakeholders, is short termist. A democracy's perception of right and wrong will seek political redress, in the form of laws and regulations, for what are seen as abuses. One spirals into a situation where these regulations in themselves spawn further abuses and further regulation, so that eventually a stranglehold is placed on enterprise and initiative. This was the danger I foresaw 10 years ago and I believe that today we are seeing such a process.

We have experienced over the past 10 years a huge increase in regulatory requirements and today because of the American scandals we are facing further legal requirements. We have had Cadbury, Greenbury, Hempel, and just recently Higgs. We now have a Financial Services Authority with greatly increased powers as well as tightening competition laws, a minimum wage and from Europe a mass of regulations on issues such as health and safety and working time. All these regulations spring from perceived abuses, whether real or otherwise. What they are doing is making it more and more difficult to maintain the freedom of enterprise, which is the surest foundation for economic prosperity and shareholder value.

Developments before and since the millennium are revealing more and more abuses not just on the other side of the Atlantic. Some of our disasters such as Marconi may have been caused by incompetence rather than knavery but they are a symptom of a deep malaise in corporate culture.

In March 1999 William Rees-Mogg wrote an article headed 'the Culture of Corruption'. It was a depressing article on the spread of dishonesty and spin in which he pointed out that, in late 18th century and early 19th century Britain, honourable people were outraged by sinecures and corruption and successfully rooted them out of British public life. This was done largely without legislation or regulation. He pointed out that for more than a century the British even ran their huge empire without bribes. He comments now that there is a new and global wave of corruption. We need a new sense of outrage, which he says is so far lacking.

Up until comparatively recently the older traditions were

common in business and the City. We had the proud boast 'my word is my bond'. I have already told on pages 138-9 the story of my negotiation with Sir Maxwell Joseph who was a member of the old school, also the chilling reaction of a close City advisor that such behaviour as Sir Maxwell's was completely out of date.

Why has this become outdated? What is the new morality and culture that says such standards are no longer appropriate? I am a great admirer of Lady Thatcher. She really did change the rules of the game, mainly for the better, but views attributed to her that 'there is no such thing as society', alongside Friedman economics and carried to extremes by such as Michael Milken with his theory 'greed is good' – admittedly he went to prison for his pains – have turned traditional standards on their head.

I place much of the blame for this in two areas – institutional investment and corporate finance. Many years of favourable tax treatment, to encourage pension provision, have led to a situation where most of British industry is actually owned by some 100 or less institutional investors, with the millions of ordinary individual shareholders only, in effect, able to be a minor irritation and embarrassment at annual general meetings. On the corporate finance side, consolidation, under the excuse of globalization, has led to a culture that accepts standards and conflicts of interest which would have been anathema to an earlier generation.

The institutional investor relies for his business on his position relative to his 'benchmark' with his peers. Even more pertinent he relies for his large bonus on beating his benchmark. Even in a falling market he expects to be paid a bonus for losing less of his customer's money than his peers.

His customers, particularly pension fund trustees, can be extremely fickle. They expect performance in the short term at least in line and woe betide if he doesn't deliver. Phillips and Drew refused to follow the technology bubble and suffered greatly at the time. Mercury Asset Management who did not have had such qualms, are now paying a heavy price in lost business because they did blow into that bubble.

There is huge pressure on companies in which the institutions invest to deliver 'Shareholder Value' however short term, even if this means, as has recently happened in several cases in America, 'cooking the books'. However the easiest and simplest way during a bull market is by deals.

Here the corporate financier comes into play. In the old days for a company to change its corporate financier was a major event. Today there is no such loyalty. In 1999 Patience Wheatcroft, City Editor of *The Times* wrote about the actions of Goldman Sachs in acting for Vodaphone against Mannesmann in a gigantic take-over battle when they had previously been advisors to Mannesmann. Commenting on corporate finance ethics she said 'The millionaires at Goldman, where even the tea boy's bonus dwarfs the national average salary, are naturally appalled by any suggestion that the firm used inside information from Mannesmann in advising Vodaphone. They do not however pretend to see why they should not take their skills and ply them on behalf of anyone who wants them and will pay for them. This is the new world of investment banks, far removed from the days when companies had long standing relationships with their advisors. They are mercenaries in Gucci loafers and Hermes ties', she concluded.

For both the institutional investor and the corporate financier, short-term shareholder value is their life's blood. It is very difficult in such an environment for any of them to look at the wider picture, and what it is doing in the longer term. It often seems that they forget that it is people out there, making widgets or beers, running pubs or hotels, that actually make the profits, in the long term, not short term wheeling and dealing.

However, so powerful is the influence of the institutional investor and corporate financier that, as happened to my own company, boards of the widget maker become so concerned not to be accused by City pundits of favouring other stakeholders, at the expense of shareholders, that they would rather close factories and asset strip a business, even when in reality it is a bad deal for shareholders. Such actions appear 'tough' and win praise in the financial press. It is perception, rather than reality, which has become so important. This in its turn has led to an explosive growth of another industry – the polite name for which is 'Public Relations' – but the more recent cynical term is 'Spin'.

In an earlier age we had advertising and marketing, and these are important to businesses in informing and persuading customers to buy their products, but in the last few years the public relations industry had developed techniques which themselves are part of the culture of corruption which so alarmed Lord Rees-Mogg. We joke cynically about it, when calling it spin, and talking about spin-doctors.

It is, I believe, extremely disturbing how spin and spin doctoring is pervading so much of modern life. How, except for a few lone voices, it is considered clever, and almost to be admired, to manipulate news, using such techniques as off the record briefings, selective leaks and non attributable sources, and deliberately being 'economical with the actuality' – in the late Alan Clark's memorable phrase.

All of this, as I forecast over ten years ago, is creating a climate which will, in the long term, become increasingly hostile to freedom of enterprise. Reaction to abuses, exacerbated by spin, have now created another virtual industry called 'Corporate Governance' – a phrase I cannot remember hearing before the nineties but which has now spawned Cadbury, then Greenbury, Higgs, etc. I believe that many of the aspects of corporate governance, far from improving the behaviour of those running companies, may actually make things worse.

Corporate governance means regulation, and regulation breeds more regulation, feeding the culture that all behaviour is acceptable provided it is within the rules. In the British case the situation is exacerbated in that the cheerleaders for corporate governance are a narrow, unelected band of City investors and financiers. The cult of short-term shareholder value is thus given a further boost, driven by a belief that any other action can only be because of a conflict of interest. On the other side, glaring conflicts of interest in corporate finance houses themselves are excused by that great myth the Chinese wall.

Institutional fund managers and corporate financiers are

individually very highly – many would say excessively – remunerated. Through their influence on corporate governance they have been very skilled at underpinning this position by persuading Cadbury, and in particularly Greenbury, to promote, as part of corporate governance, that highly inflationary board committee, now almost mandatory, the remuneration committee.

While there was always envy of fat cats, there was no serious problem with the levels of executive pay until remuneration committees became the norm. I remember reading in the early 1980s the statement, from a prominent trade unionist, that it was totally wrong for anyone to be paid less than the average – just think about that. Think of inflationary leapfrogging to get there. How often nowadays do we read in annual reports statements by a remuneration committee chairman, along the lines of 'we employ the best and pay in The Upper Quartile'.

There are numerous firms of remuneration consultants now advising remuneration committees and producing statistics showing deciles, quartiles, medians, averages and norms. What remuneration committee dare recommend payment of less than the median, average or norm to the company's management, particularly when the members of these committees are so often drawn from the management of other plcs. Is it surprising that executive directors reward inflation is so high and often so unrelated to performance?

This is fuelling the politics of envy and even revulsion. The reaction to this will be political and will catch not just the unworthy but inhibit proper reward for those who really have earned it.

I believe that people have lost sight of what is right and what is wrong. Instead we have spin and perception. Too many managements are so concerned to pacify their 'City' owners by delivering so called 'Shareholder Value', even when this may be spurious, that they do not look at the reality or the longer term. In the Vaux case it was easier to take the 'tough decision' of closing the breweries and throwing hundreds out of work, thus winning the plaudits of Lex and other commentators, than to listen to the advice I was giving, because the 'perception' was that I must have a conflict of interest.

It was an impossible position for me. If I had gone, the new Chief Executive abetted by BTAB would have had little difficulty bamboozling his colleagues to close the breweries. By staying I provoked the self-righteousness of certain institutions displaying the prejudices which the article I have referred to earlier by Graham Searjeant of April 8 1999 talked about, when he referred to 'City fund managers who hate family dynasties with a passion that reminds you of Robespierre'. The likes of Hermes so pressurized the board that the easy and short term way out was to take the so called 'tough' decision of brewery closure. This was not the 'tough' decision at all. I still maintain that if my former colleagues had had the guts to face down certain shareholders, these shareholders would never have faced the public opprobrium that would have been their lot in voting for brewery closure.

Unmodified Friedmanism is short termist, but it is or, certainly at the time of the Vaux closure, it was the gospel of the City of London among most of the major institutions who own so much of British industry, and among the huge array of corporate financiers and analysts, spin doctors and media, who feed off them.

I accept that shareholder value should be paramount. I do not for instance believe that it is necessarily admirable for companies to make charitable donations, unless that donation in some way improves the business climate and thus profit for that company.

I do however believe that leaders of business and finance need to be aware, collectively and individually, of the effects of their actions and that, unless they are seen to behave fairly and honourably, they tarnish the whole cause of business and this, in the longer term, inevitably destroys shareholder value.

If we look back at the history of the last 100 years, we can see how the pendulum has swung between freedom of enterprise and state control. Each swing is caused by excess. The laissez-faire of the late 19th and early 20th centuries led to the granting of excessive legal power to trade unions, then to nationalization and socialism. The excesses this produced and the economic damage it caused in turn led to the revolution of the 1980s.

For those of us who had cut our teeth in business in the sixties and seventies, it was almost unbelievable what happened. Suddenly we were given back the power to manage. The power of the unions was rolled back. We were given the opportunity to earn reward with top rate taxes falling from 98% to 40% It was almost unbelievable good fortune at the time. It is scarcely credible to the current generation that the world of the seventies with such taxes, with the three-day week and the winter of discontent, could have ever existed. However the freedoms we were given did not bring responsibility. In the 1990s we have seen too many abuses of these freedoms. Too often individual and corporate greed has been shown.

I am concerned about the future. What we are seeing today is a swing back of the pendulum towards state control and suppression of enterprise, under an increasing burden of regulation and taxation. This cannot be good. Sadly I can see little sign that revulsion to the abuses to what has been happening is provoking the same reaction William Rees-Mogg talked about as happened in the early 19th century. There is no clear code emerging of 'personal governance' and an understanding of what is right and what is wrong. Instead we have corporate governance with more and more laws and regulations – good for lawyers but in the longer term disastrous for wealth creating enterprise and initiative.

Appendix 1

Summary of Numbers in BTAB Paper Sent to Board on 19th March 1999

THE FIRST PAGE of numbers listed ten alternatives to the MBO. It had four columns, the first headed 'Capital Value to the Group' and the second 'Discounted Effect on Group Profits at 7% Discount'. The first two columns were then totalled in the third column and the fourth column showed the variance from the MBO offer. The first three columns each had a sub heading 'Mid value'.

In Column 1 the 'Mid value' of the management offer was taken as £63.7 million and the value of the alternatives ranged between £58.3 million and £71.9 million.

In Column 2 the 'Mid value' of the management offer was taken as £5.8 million and the value of the alternatives ranged between £11.5 million and £21.3 million.

The alternatives with a 'Higher value' in Column 1 tended to have a 'Lower value' in Column 2. However BTAB's paper purported to show that all the ten alternatives were better than the management offer by between £8.6 million and £15.4 million.

All of the alternatives were based on a 'Mid value' from an asset strip of the Breweries of £31.4 million.

The second page showed how the £31.4 million was arrived at. The page was headed 'Brewery Closure – Option Evaluation' and the final three columns headed 'Realisation Value', showed a 'Low' a 'Mid' and a 'High'. £31.4 million was the 'Mid' figure. The paper purported to analyse in detail the likely realisations from disposal of the assets of the Breweries and the costs of closure. It applied a discount factor of 10% per year from timing and assumed in the 'Mid figure' it would take two and a half years to sell Sunderland, two years to sell Sheffield and an average of one year to sell the plant.

The paper netted against the asset sales a forecast of costs and associated tax recoveries and showed besides the 'Mid figure' of £31.4 million a 'Low' of £28.6 million and a 'High' of £37.6 million. *Appendix 5 shows that the actual realisation was probably only £16.1 million.*

Appendix 2

Swallow Group

Memo to: All Board Members | From: Chairman
Date: 22nd March 1999

PROJECT TANKARD

I think I should clarify the position as I see it.

A. Within the Company:

1. The MBO and their backers have reached their final position.
2. We are now in a position where one of our joint advisers believes that their offer is recommendable to shareholders and the other does not. We have probably two members of the sale committee who, if both advisers recommend acceptance, would feel comfortable. We have a third member who is unhappy with the offer's supply terms but, so far as I can identify, would feel more comfortable if there was £1.7m more value to the Group (representing a recovery of what he believes is the excess value given by the tying arrangements).
3. Numbers have been prepared by one set of advisers purporting to show that alternatives – all of which involve closure – are up to £15.4m better for the Group. No consideration is being given to alternative strategies, not involving closure. £15.4m represents 10.5p per share, or 3.9% of the Group's current market cap. The Group's share price has oscillated over the period since the initial approach on July 10th, 1998, between 360p and 190p.
4. There is another view that the numbers prepared by this adviser overestimate the actual benefit of closure options by at least £12m and probably much more – before any account is taken of intangible damage to customer goodwill and the

problems that alternatives would cause to management.

5. It is inevitable in the nearly nine months that the process has taken (over four months since the submission of final offers) that the business is under threat of falling apart. Normal management, particularly in the area of communication of what is happening, has not been permitted. Morale is sinking rapidly and value is being destroyed.
6. There could be justifiable criticism levelled at the Group for mismanagement following their requirement of a final submission of offers on 20th November. Initially this was caused by the former Chief Executive, subsequently it is because of the way negotiations have been handled, with so many different directors and advisers involved. Positions have constantly changed. Points have been agreed with the other party then subsequently vetoed because another director or adviser did not accept them.
7. In the remaining Group businesses, a major part is still performing well, in spite of top managers' attention being distracted. Unless, however, there is a quick and clean exit from brewing, through the offer on the table, there is a real danger of significant damage to the ongoing business if closure is being implemented or even being prepared for. This is not least because of the problems for the executive of managing an extremely messy process in the full glare of hostile publicity.
8. There can be hardly any parallel where a plant closure has occurred when the board has had a reasonable offer from the management. The argument that this offer is unique in relying on a supply contract (albeit limited as to time and quantity) does not stack up. Frequently MBOs maintain close relations with their parents who are often investors in the MBO and it is by no means uncommon for these to be reflected by ongoing contracts. Bass's relationship with Tradeteam would be an example.
9. While the process continues, 700 families continue to worry about their future.

External Factors

1. A disastrous appointment was made by the Group of a Chief Executive who had no concept of Group responsibility or feel for the drinks business's principal trading area.
2. This Chief Executive had determined at an early stage that the breweries should be closed regardless of the arguments. The Finance Director supported him in this.
3. When the other eight directors did not accept their view, the Chief Executive and Finance Director went behind the backs of the colleagues direct to major shareholders with numbers purporting to show a benefit of £23.3m from closure.
4. When the Chief Executive and Finance Director were sacked, certain major shareholders queried the corporate governance of the Group, and apparently continue to believe that the board, if they recommend the offer, will not be behaving properly.
5. Non executive directors are extremely nervous that if they recommend the offer this would be rejected by shareholders.
6. There is very strong local and regional, not to say national, support for the breweries. Of the 12,000 shareholders, I would suspect an overwhelming majority, when presented with the facts, would want the MBO to succeed.
7. Directors and advisers, who are not familiar with the region, underestimate the popular and political fallout when it becomes known that they may be favouring options that give the breweries no future. The influence of the region in government is strong. Almost certainly there would be heavy, if not irresistible, calls for regulatory investigation, particularly because there is powerful evidence of predatory pricing. Any investigation would cause further major uncertainties for the company.
8. A closure threat could become a 'cause celebre', defining the limits of board and shareholder responsibilities to stakeholders and others. In these circumstances, the position of individuals involved would inevitably be highlighted. There would be heroes and villains.
9. If the board were to recommend the offer, I believe that any

shareholder revolt would quickly evaporate. Who would want to face the political and public heat that would be turned on those seeking to throw 700 people in Sunderland and Sheffield onto the dole. Anyway, surely investors' priority must be to conclude this matter so that there is certainty in operating the business.

Summary

If the breweries were to have no future, there would be three areas of responsibility for this.

1. Certain City institutions owning shares in the business of which the Post Office pension fund, Hermes, has been the most vociferous. They have chosen to condone grossly improper behaviour by two former directors who were sacked and seek to interfere in the decision-making process of the board, with threats and requirements, which have made sensible and proper management and governance of a successful and profitable company almost impossible. What a pass has been reached when, because one director is married to the Chairman's wife's sister, and another is a former employee, they are precluded from the process!
2. The adviser and others who do not feel able to recommend the MBO. In the case of the adviser concerned, I think there is a serious lack of comprehension of the position and interests of their client. As an example, I was told by one of their team that it was assumed that announcement and closure would be more or less simultaneous and no account need be or indeed has been taken in modelling, of loss of profit during run down. Being charitable, I suppose that if an individual's experience is largely limited to the Square Mile, one can see how such a belief could be held.

   I have, as is known, serious and continuing reservations about the validity of the model that this adviser has been using, both as to its assumptions and because of the frequent errors in the many revisions that have been made. Recent examples of errors are miscalculations of the effect of fifteen-day credit and of the timing of price increases. Almost all of the assumptions and the bulk of the errors, before correction, have overstated the comparative benefits of its other options to the offer. Primarily, the model is totally unrealistic in its assessment of the costs and realisations on closure.

Once a closure process started the flaws in the model would quickly become apparent, but by then it would be too late. I do believe that this adviser needs to look again very carefully at the consequences of its current advice.

So far as others are concerned, should £1.7m of value (1.2p per share) really be the straw that breaks the camel's back?

3. Those members of the sale committee, who would like to believe the other adviser that the offer is a solution which can be recommended to shareholders, but are fearful of making such a recommendation because they feel it would be voted down by shareholders.

Conclusions

People have said that I am biased. I am. I am biased towards ensuring best value for our shareholders, and it should not be forgotten that I am personally a substantial one. The offer achieves this value. If other shareholders were to disagree, and reject this, let them run the company. In the meantime, as a board, we should do what is right and principled.

I must give each of you notice that if this cannot be accepted, and serious consideration is being given to the other alternatives in the current model, then I may have to exercise my fundamental right and duty to shareholders to dissent by public comment on this position and the competence of the procedures which have led to this position. It will of course be your privilege to decide what action you may wish to take in such circumstances, in accordance with the Articles of Association of the company.

In all of this I assume you will indicate to shareholders, through the press and other means, the precise figures which you believe will be achievable as a result of adopting these alternatives and that you will put these to shareholders, not least to establish that this whole process has been conducted with proper diligence.

APPENDIX 3

Jonathan Cartwright Esq FCA
Caledonia Investments plc
Cayzer House
1 Thomas More Street
London
E1 9AR.

22nd July 1999

(Dear Jonathan)
It was nice to have a brief chat with you on Thursday, although it was a far from happy occasion. I am writing to you as you were Chairman of the sale committee on 19th March and also because you, like me, are a member of a distinguished professional body.

I attach:

1. The Journal's account of Peter Catesby's statement to the EGM on 15th July, which accords with my own recollection of what he said.
2. The page from Bankers Trust's paper of 18th March 1999 presented to the board on 19th March, purporting to evaluate the closure options against the MBO.
3. The page from the same paper headed 'Brewery Closure Option Evaluation'.
4. Letter from the MBO's backers, Alchemy, to BT Alex Brown (BT), dated 31st March 1999.

As I shall explain, I believe you, as a professional man, should find what Peter revealed and claimed in his statement to the EGM, deeply disturbing.

If we take Attachment 1 as an accurate record of what was said, then we should look at Attachment 2. It was on the basis of this analysis that the sale committee chaired by you, felt unable to recommend proceeding with the MBO because there were, apparently, options available which would mean a substantially greater value gap between the MBO and closure than the £10 million the board were prepared to accept. The paper showed gaps in value under various options of up to £15.4 million.

A major part of the calculations behind the analysis of all these options was the estimate that an asset strip of the breweries would yield £31.4 million (Attachment 3 – orange highlight). As you will recall, *I repeatedly drew to your attention and to BT's, what I regarded as very serious flaws in the model* that I believed over estimated the likely realisation by between £10-£15 million.

Peter revealed (Attachment 1 – page 2 highlighted) that what is actually likely to be realised after selling the pubs for £127.5 million and valuing the remaining tenancies at £12 million, is only a net extra of £14 million, making up his total of £153.5 million. Of course some of the difference apparently £1.5 million, may relate to costs associated with sale of the pubs but this would still leave a gap of £15.9 million between what BT modelled would be achieved (£31.4 million) from the asset strip and what Peter is now saying will be realised. I am not privy to calculations on tax, timing or indeed reduction of profit during run down which could affect the numbers, however, it is absolutely clear that *as I warned you at the time*, BT's model on which you based the tragic decision announced on 23rd March has proved grossly flawed. An estimate in their model of a net realisation from working capital of £2.9 million (Attachment 3 – yellow highlight) turns out to be £8.9 million overstated. Estimated closure costs of £18.3 million (Attachment 3 – pink highlight) turn out to be some £5 million understated, subject to what may actually have been allocated to the pubs.

We now come onto the 'spin' being put out that somehow what has been achieved is '£30 million better than the management's final offer'. I don't know whether you have read the letter from Alchemy to BT of 31st March (Attachment 4). You will note that this letter was sent 8 days after the 23rd March date when, as Swallow's disposal document discloses, negotiations with the management had been terminated.

There can however be no source for the 'spin' other than the paragraphs from this letter, highlighted on page 2. To interpret what the letter calls 'A more radical approach which we would be prepared to explore with you' as a final offer from the MBO is in my view misleading to the point of misrepresentation to shareholders.

I hope no one will seek to salve his or her conscience by alleging the MBO should have bid for the 8th April package. After the way the MBO had been treated, they and their backers reckoned that the board had another agenda. You may remember a statement was made to the press about Alchemy's letter of 31st March before the MBO had even received the courtesy of a reply. In any case, the goodwill value of the brewing business had been fatally compromised by Swallow's public announcements of 23rd March and 1st April.

Of course the tragedy that has occurred is now history. However, those who remain on the board even if they have no social conscience, should reflect on their own judgement and competence as well as that of the adviser, BT Alex Brown.

I would be interested in your comments, as the one professional man among the members of the board at the time of my resignation.

(Yours sincerely)
(Sir Paul Nicholson)

c.c. Swallow Group plc Board Members

Appendix 3A

Summary of Attachments to Sir Paul Nicholson's Letter of 22nd July 1999 to J. Cartwright

1. The Journal's account of Peter Catesby's statement to the EGM on 15th July 1999.

   During the meeting Swallow Chief Executive Peter Catesby said the MBO's final offer of £125m for the breweries and pubs 'fell well short of the value being offered by alternative routes'.

   He produced figures to show proceeds of £30m more than the MBO offer will be realised by the steps being taken by the board.

   Mr Catesby said the £125m being paid by Pubmaster was 'an excellent price, in line with the best values being realised for tenancies in the market'.

   'We intend to retain 41 properties with a value of £12m which have the potential to be converted into managed houses . . . The free trade loan book will realise around £19m and we expect beer raising equipment we are selling to Bass produce a further £2m'.

   The sale of the Waggle Dance beer brand to Youngs of London and Scorpian Lager to Wolverhampton and Dudley, will together bring £500,000.

   A valuation of £13m has been put on the Vaux site in Sunderland, £300,000 on the depot in the city and £2m for the Sheffield site.

   Another depot in Rochdale has been sold for £1.2m, while the sale of brewery plant, transport and equipment will raise at least £5m.

'Taking away the cost of closure, fees and contingencies which are in the region of £23m, and a loss on working capital of £6m, that makes a total of £153.5m, some £30.5m more than the buy-out's £125m which, after fees, was worth £123m'.

He said: 'The disposal of the tenancies marks the end of the transformation of the Swallow Group into a company focused on two core businesses: hotels and pubs and restaurants.'

2. The page from Bankers Trust's paper of 18th March 1999 presented to the board on 19th March, purporting to evaluate the closure options against the MBO.

   This has been summarised in Appendix 1.
3. The page from the same paper headed 'Brewery Closure Option Evaluation'.

   This has also been summarised in Appendix 1.
4. Letter from the MBO's backers, Alchemy, to BT Alex Brown (BT), dated 31st March 1999.

   The relevant extract is:

   A more radical approach, which we would be prepared to explore with you, is set out below. This would inevitably lengthen the process but we would be happy to progress this during the finalisation of Options 1 or 2 if it were of interest and your timescale allowed it. However, it is essential that any discussions with the DTI take place very soon if there is to be any prospect of saving the business, a prerequisite of which is agreement between the parties.

Option 3

- Inclusion of all remaining Swallow tenancies
- No supply contract
- Increase in price from £62.9m to an indicative £125m (including working capital at the levels incorporated in the original offer). Subject to satisfactory confirmatory due diligence

All options necessitate the satisfactory transfer of the Carling and other brewing agreements.

The current uncertainty surrounding the status of the transaction is undoubtedly having a rapid and material adverse impact on the operation of the business, which will soon become unsustainable. I would therefore request a prompt response to our proposals, and in any case no later than 5pm on Tuesday 6 April. We are prepared to meet with the Sale Committee at any time if that would be of assistance.

Yours sincerely
Paul Bridges, Partner

Appendix 3B

Reply by J.H. Cartwright to Sir Paul Nicholson's letter of 22nd July 1999

23rd August, 1999

Dear Paul,

I am in receipt of your letter dated 22nd July, 1999, together with attachments, which I note has been circulated to Swallow board members.

In responding to your comments, I do not believe that any benefit can be derived from a detailed re-examination of the assumptions and valuations which formed a part of the financial model utilised by the sale committee in its task of forming a view as to whether to recommend the MBO. Judgmental areas, such as net values of site realisations and plant disposals, will only be proven in the light of future events.

In your letter you make mention of 'spin' and of the board having a set agenda other than (as I interpret your comments) allowing the MBO a fair assessment. You also appear to imply a lack of social conscience on the board's part and to question board members 'judgement and competence'. You have made public allegations of 'corporate vandalism'. Your letter also questions the competence of BT Alex Brown and, in particular, the integrity of their financial model.

Throughout the process the sale committee had the utmost confidence in the integrity and independence of the advice from BT Alex Brown. You will recall that Noble Grossart, co-advisers with BT Alex Brown, agreed with BT Alex Brown's advice and raised no objections to the financial model.

I am satisfied with the basis of all relevant deliberations, and for you to imply anything other than honourable and competent conduct by board members is, in my view, an unfounded criticism of those who have worked with you and provided loyal support over many years. As I am sure you will appreciate, the members of the sale committee together with all other board members involved, view such unfounded criticism very seriously.

I believe that, whatever further examination or discussion there might be about the basis for the recent recommendations by the board, which have now been approved by shareholders, you will not agree with the actions taken. Nothing constructive can be achieved by your current course of action and I therefore urge you in the interests of the Swallow Group and its employees both past and present, to cease this campaign.

Yours sincerely
J.H. Cartwright

Appendix 3C

J H Cartwright Esq
Caledonia Investments plc
Cayzer House
1 Thomas More Street
London
E1 9AR.

25th August 1999

(Dear Jonathan)
Thank you for your letter of 23rd August 1999 in response to mine of 22nd July.

Sadly, but not unexpectedly, your letter fails to address any of the substantive points I made. I realise that to do so would be difficult without admitting that you may have been wrong and made a tragic mistake when you refused to listen to what I repeatedly told you at the time, that the numbers in the model were very flawed. Most of your letter is frankly bluster. Of the criticisms of your actions you read into my letter, some were not made, the rest are very well founded on the facts, particularly those revealed in the enclosures that accompanied my letter, which you do not appear to have taken in.

You refer, however, in the final paragraph to an alleged 'campaign'. There is no such campaign. The closure of the breweries is history. The value destroyed and the misery caused can now rest only on the commercial and social consciences of those responsible. I would not sleep easily at night if I had been one of them.

I note you copied your letter to the rest of the board. I leave it to you whether you wish to copy them with this response.

(Yours ever)
(Paul)

Appendix 4

Bishop's Address

The Vaux Brewery Thanksgiving Service
Sunderland Minster – 21 June 1999

I EXPECT THAT in the past the attitudes of worshippers at this church towards the presence of the Brewery around the corner would have been at least as strong as the smells emanating from the Brewery until decent filtration methods were introduced. I dread to think what late 19th Century vestrymen would have thought about the Bishop of Durham speaking at a thanksgiving service for the unregenerate enemy of temperance. I am surprised that there has been no ghostly picket of Rekabites.

In fact, the Bible is altogether silent on the subject of beer. Drunkenness and wine bibbing are roundly and rightly condemned, not least because of their being so closely linked with violence, promiscuity and the escape from responsibility. The Church has, however shown its confidence in the healthy properties of ale and beer by having breweries of its own: Bishop's Finger and Abbots Ale are not a coincidence. We take safe and clean drinking water for granted, but this is a very recent development. For a good deal of human history, it has been safer for people to drink weak beer with breakfast. Those who fought for the Temperance Movement were really concerned about the devastating effect of cheap and fiery spirits upon those already in the grip of desperate poverty.

Not that I am suggesting for a moment that Vaux has produced weak or watery ale. We are here to celebrate well over 150 years during which many fine brews have been developed, savoured and exported. When the Brewery was formed, the Industrial Revolution was gathering pace and transforming Sunderland's manufacturing, mining and engineering industries. Until very recently, you could be warmed or powered by Sunderland coal, look through a lens made from Sunderland glass, travel in a ship built on the Wear, produce tools and goods from Sunderland machinery. With Vaux beers, you could also savour the taste of Sunderland.

So let us join in uninhibited thanksgiving for the years in which Vaux has served this city and its forerunners. In our reading, Jesus said 'Seek ye first the Kingdom of God'. No human institution perfectly mirrors God's ideal, but there are features of Vaux history, which comply with many of the parables in which Jesus of Nazareth described the characteristics of his Kingdom. Let me mention briefly just four of them.

First, the profit motive and the creation of wealth is the foundation of much of industrial and economic activities. There is nothing wrong in principle with this, so long as it is seen in the context of the whole of Jesus' teaching. Going for the largest profit at the price of justice and the common good, He would roundly condemn. But wealth for the common good and not for personal greed He would welcome.

Secondly, Jesus commended the creation of honest work. This fulfils the Biblical understanding of man and his relationship to God and the dignity of man in the image of God. That is why institutionalised unemployment is regarded as an evil.

Thirdly, Jesus commends the sharing of prosperity. In any large business this would include the shareholders, the Board members, all employees and, of course, the customers. Each of them has rights and also responsibilities and a successful company will see that both are exercised. Recognising the rights of others may sometime demand the sacrifice of some of our own rights and the exercise of power which economic success brings, must always be done in utter fairness and with an eye to the needs of others and their rights as human beings.

Fourthly, a business which is worthy of the name of success, will be one which cultivates the care of all that are involved in the industry. In the Vaux and Sunderland context I must express the great debt that we all owe to several generations of the Nicholson family. It was them who not only built up a successful business, but made sure that its breweries had a caring and family atmosphere about them. Many of the people who work at Vaux have counted it a privilege to do so simply because they have caught the inspiration and the fair-minded leadership of successive generations of Nicholsons. Moreover, the spirit has been infectious and I have been glad to meet a number of people working at Vaux who are themselves the current expression of their own long family traditions. Not only skills have been passed down from generation to generation, but an understanding of the way in which Vaux works and in which it has succeeded not only in building a business, but one which it was good and enjoyable to work for.

We must keep all these things in mind as we think of the use of the site and the land which will become available when the Brewery closes. For the sake of the City of Sunderland we need to make sure that what goes on such a strategic site in the heart of the city is a creative influence in people's lives, has a community consciousness about it and provides a framework in which the principles of care can be expressed. Though brewing may cease, so much of what Vaux has stood for should continue on that site. Then, though the brewing goes we shall discharge the obligations which its noble history bequeaths to us.

Any great city must honour its history and recognise the enterprise and values which formed it. But the past must not be an anchor which keeps us in port. Rather let the things of which we are justly proud be the sails which enable us to catch the fresh winds of opportunity which will carry us into the future.

Michael Turnbull
Bishop of Durham

APPENDIX 5

Closure of Vaux and Wards Breweries

Decision based on wrong estimates of over £15m

Following the sale of the Sunderland Brewery site by Swallow Group's owners Whitbread completed on 1 March 2002, it is now possible to assess the out-turn against the estimates on which the decision to close Vaux Brewery in Sunderland and Wards Brewery in Sheffield was based. The analysis shows that the estimates appear wrong by at least £15 million.

The destruction was authorised by the Board of Swallow Group plc on the basis of figures prepared by a London Corporate Financier that this would achieve up to £15 million more value for shareholders than accepting an offer from Management to buy and operate the Breweries which employed over 550.

The decision was announced on 23 March 1999. Subsequently the Board sought to explain by claiming that they would have accepted the management offer if the difference in expected value had been less than £10 million. This was because of unquantifiable goodwill costs from closing the Breweries

For some weeks before I resigned on 26 March 1999 I had been pointing out to the Board that I believed the numbers being produced by the Corporate Financier were very flawed. In my final memo to the Board of 22 March 1999 I said that these were wrong by over £12 million.

In my resignation statement of 26 March 1999 I said...

> Having tried my hardest to convince the generality of my Board colleagues that to break off negotiations with the breweries MBO team, with the near inevitable closure of the Sunderland and Sheffield breweries and the loss of over 700 jobs, in an area of already high unemployment, was against the interests of the shareholders (of whom I am one for a substantial proportion of my net worth), the time has come to resign.

> I remain convinced that the financial shortfall of the MBO offer is overstated and, in reality, de minimis in the context of Swallow's market capitalisation of almost £400 million.

There was a claim made at an EGM of the Swallow Group on 15 July 1999 to approve the sale of the tenanted pubs that what was achieved by such a sale delivered £30 million more value than the management's final offer This claim was grossly misleading as no comparable offer was ever made by the management team. However by the time of the EGM it was apparent to me that the numbers the Board had accepted in so far as they could be identified were already very wrong.

On pointing this out I received a reply from the Chairman of the Committee of the Board which had recommended closure stating inter alia

> I do not believe that any benefit can be derived from a detailed reexamination of the assumptions and valuations which formed part of the financial model utilised by the Sale Committee in its task of forming a view as to whether to recommend the MBO. Judgemental areas such as net values of site realisation and plant disposals will only be proven in the light of future events.

Following the sale of the Sunderland Brewery site the Sales Committees 'Future Events' of July 1999 are now in the past. The Corporate Financier had estimated an asset strip of the Breweries would yield £31.393 million. It may actually have yielded only £16.147m. The detailed calculation and reasonings are in the analyses.

Eight months after I resigned the Board accepted an offer for what remained of the company of £3.98 per share, some 40 times the price in 1974 when I effectively began my stewardship. In the circumstances shareholders have not themselves suffered much damage from the closure of the Breweries. However it remains a fact that the destruction of Vaux and Wards Breweries has been a tragedy for Sunderland and Sheffield. It certainly raises questions as to the competence and quality of judgement of those responsible.

Analyses of Estimates against out-turn of asset realisations and costs relating to the closure of Vaux and Wards Breweries

Below is a summary and attached are details with notes of how the out-turn numbers are arrived at. It is not possible without an audit to be fully accurate on some of the numbers. Following the sale of Swallow to Whitbread this is not feasible. However where the numbers cannot be ascertained accurately I have taken a conservative view.

I wrote to the then Chairman of Swallow in January 2000 following publication of Swallow accounts with an analysis showing errors at that stage on the face of these accounts of £12.2 million. I had at that time assumed that the costs of early retirement granted to some 112 employees had been included. However I discovered subsequently that this was not the case. These costs had actually been subsumed into an actuarial surplus in the pension fund. Note 8 explains the reasonings and calculations used to assess these. They are of course just as much 'costs' as those charged in the accounts.

Summary

Estimates of March 1999 (taken from 'Mid column' of Brewery closure – option evaluation document)		Out-turn	
	£000s	£000s	
Asset realisations	41305	36711	Note 1
Costs	9912	20564	Note 2
Total	31393	16147	
Difference	£15,246		

Sir Paul Nicholson 18 March 2002

ASSET REALISATIONS

COMPARISONS OF ESTIMATE AT 19 MARCH 1999 WITH OUT-TURNS (Note 1)

Realisations	**19 March 1999 Estimate £000**	**Out-turn £000**	**Better/(Worse) £000**	**Reference**
Loans	21500	17398	(4102)	Note 3
Net working capital	2851	(420)	(3271)	Note 4
Plant & equipment	5393	4300	(1093)	Note 5
Brands	0	885	885	Note 6
Properties	11561	14548	2987	Note 7
TOTAL	**41305**	**36711**	**(4594)**	

COSTS OF CLOSURE

(All figures are £000s unless otherwise stated)

COMPARISON OF ESTIMATES AT 19 MARCH 1999 WITH OUT-TURNS (Note 2)

Costs	**March 1999 Estimates**	**Actual**	**Difference**	**Reference**
Severance Costs				
Redundancy	9470			
Notice pay	1560			
Directors notice pay	464			
Outplacement services	300	11967	(173)	Per Swallow Accounts 1999
Costs of early retirement charged to Pension fund at £34.9 per head on 112 employees	0	3909	(3909)	Note 8
SUB TOTAL	**11794**	**15876**	**(4082)**	
Costs of run down	0	807	(807)	Per Swallow Accounts 1999
Onerous contracts & legal fees	5245	7046	(1801)	Per Swallow Accounts 1999
Site clearance costs	625	125	500	Note 9
Site security, insurance and skeleton staff	580	580	0	Site Manager said estimates were about right
Costs of accountancy & debt collection	0	463	(463)	Note 10
Moving of equipment, computers etc	0	500	(500)	Note 11
Tax recoverable	(8332)	(4833)	(3499)	Note 12
TOTAL	**9912**	**20564**	**10652**	

		Figures £000			
Note 3	**Realisation of Loans** **£000** Swallow's September 1999 account showed a net book value before write offs of £25,163 as opposed to £25,820 in the Corporate Financier's estimates. The difference is what was achieved between the time of the estimate and Brewery closure and is included in the total achieved column which is a balancing figure after the known write offs which consist of Per September 1999 accounts £6,642. Subsequent events and loans put back to Whitbread by Bass of a gross £1220 sold on for £420 and £3500 sold at a discount of approximately £1000 to Interbrew.	Estimate (write off) Out-turn	£4320 £8422	Worse	(£4102)
Note 4	**Stock Debtors and Prepayments** Swallow accounts of September 1999 showed a gross of £18,962 and a write down of £4,771. The Corporate Financier's estimates showed a net of £2,851 after a write down of £1,500.	Estimate (write down) Out-turn	£1500 £4771	Worse	(£3271)
Note 5	**Plant Equipment** Information I have from those involved is that net of fees the plant has raised £4300 which is £1093 worse than the Corporate Financier's estimate.	Estimate (realisation) Out-turn	£5393 £4300	Worse	(£1093)
Note 6	**Brands** There was no allowance for Brands in the Corporate Financier's estimate. They have realised £885 made up as shown. Samson to Federation (2001) £400 Waggle Dance to Youngs (1999) £300 Scorpion to Wolv & Dudley (1999) £100 Double Maxim to former exec (2000) £70 Lorimers to Caledonian (2001) £15	Estimate Out-turn	0 £885	Better	£885

Note	Item	Figures £000			
Note 7	**Properties**				
7 (a)	**Sunderland** The Sunderland site has been sold by Whitbread to Tesco on 1 March 2002 for sums variously reported as £12000 and £12300. I have taken £12300 and I have also added £1000 for the value of the former garage site, which is probably high. Reportedly this was not in the sale to Tesco. This makes a total of £13300 achieved after 35 months. I have applied the same discounting for time factor to the price as in the estimate, which was for a sale receiving £500 immediately and £9500 after 30 months. The Sunderland site therefore has achieved on this basis £10573 compared to an estimate of £8380 and this is better by £2193	Estimate Out-turn	£8380 £10573	Better	£2193
7 (b)	**Sheffield** An announcement was made that the Sheffield site had been sold for £3700. This appears to have been 20 months after the announcement as opposed to an estimate of £2300 after 24 months. The difference is a favourable £1264 against the estimate.	Estimate Out-turn	£1901 £3165	Better	£1264
7 (c)	**Riverside Road** This was sold for £200 against an estimate of £425 after 12 months giving a net estimate of £386. I have not made any timing deductions on the out-turn.	Estimate Out-turn	£386 £200	Worse	(£186)
7 (d)	**Rochdale** This was sold for £950 against an estimate £1100 no timing difference has been taken either on the estimate or out-turn.	Estimate Out-turn	£1100 £950	Worse	(£150)
7 (e)	**Expenses** These were estimated at 2% of Sunderland and Sheffield proceeds. The estimate for which was £12300 and the out-turn £17000.	Estimate Out-turn	£206 £340	Worse	(£134)

SUMMARY OF PROPERTY SALES

	Estimated Gross £m	After Timing £m	Achieved Gross £m	After Timing £m
Sunderland	£10	£8.380	£13.3	£10.573
Sheffield	£2.3	£1.901	£3.7	£3.165
Riverside Road	£.425	£.386	£.2	£.2
Rochdale	£1.1	£1.100	£.950	£.950
	£12.825		£18.150	
Expenses		(.206)		(.340)
		£11.561		£14.548

Note 8 **Early Retirement Costs**

Employees at 50 in the Senior Staff Scheme (normal retirement 60) and 55 in the Brewery Scheme (normal retirement 65) were offered the opportunity to take a reduced redundancy package plus a pension with no reduction for early retirement (which otherwise would have been 4%pa). This offer was attractive to those eligible with more than 5 years to go to normal retirement but those with less than 5 years to go were likely to be better off taking the full redundancy package.

I understand 112 employees took this package. I do not know the balance between senior staff and others but I have assumed that the average recipient was retiring at 54 for senior staff and 59 for employees. To even out between staff and employees I have taken the value of the premium to be 28% equivalent to 7 years early. The pension payable had a 50% spouse benefit together with an R.P.I element capped at 5% pa. I have taken £17,000 as the average salary (probably low) and 22 years as the average length of service (20 plus years was the average for all). On this basis the early retirement 'benefit' was £1745 pa per head. The early retirement benefit to some senior staff was much higher, the Head Brewers benefit was over £11,000 pa drawn at age 53 with an actuarial cost of over £250,000 for him alone. However on the above basis an annuity drawn at age 58 would have an initial rate of around 5%. This gives a capital cost per head of £34,900 and a total cost of £3.909 million. This may well be low.

Similar terms were subsequently offered to others made redundant by the tenancy sales and the takeover of the company. I would strongly suspect that the scheme which may have had an actuarial surplus at April 1999 will now under FRS17 be in substantial deficit exacerbated by these early retirements and also large salary increases granted to certain Directors. One must hope that Whitbread or successor companies will be able and willing to honour obligations to former Vaux employees which may stretch many decades into the future.

Figures £000			
Estimate	nil		
Out-turn	£3909		
		Worse	(£3909)

		Figures £000			
Note 9	**Site Clearance Costs** Whitbread did not clear the site before they sold it however they incurred costs of demolition to extract plant of £65,000 and costs of £60,000 from the abortive start to demolition where they removed the bottling hall roof, discovered Asbestos and then just left a roofless building which remains a terrible eyesore near the centre of the city.	Estimate Out-turn	£625 £125	Better	£500
Note 10	**Cost of Accountancy and Debt Collection** Whitbread continued to pay substantial consultancy fees for debt collection and accountancy after September 1999 now confirmed at £463,000.	Estimate Out-turn	nil £463	Worse	(£463)
Note 11	**Moving of Equipment and Computers etc** I am informed that moving the computer etc cost £1 million. The management had offered to accommodate remaining Group computer and other needs. The closure of the site meant that the computer move had to be expedited. At least half of this cost is a direct result of the decision.	Estimate Out-turn	nil £500	Worse	(£500)
Note 12	**Tax Recoverable** **£000** Per Accounts to September 1999 £4247 Per Accounts to March 2000 (described as credit relating to exceptional items) £364 Per Accounts to March 2001 (description adjustment to earlier periods) £222	Estimate recovery Out-turn	£8332 £4833	Worse	(£3499)

Index